To: P

Thank,

Prayers

Gateway to Iraq:
A Chaplain's Story

—ɯ—

Rachel Coggins
Chaplain, United States Army Reserves

... by the grace of God

Rachel Coggins

www.xulonpress.com

Dedicated to those who have died to give us the freedom to live. May we live boldly and honorably so as to show our gratitude for your sacrifice.

To the brave men, women and family members who make up the American and coalition forces.

To my loving husband who supports me in all things. You are the wind beneath my wings.

Table of Contents

—w—

0000 — Introduction: Battle Rhythm

—ᴡ—

The Gateway is the name of a small base in Kuwait where each day an average of 1,400 service members passed through on their way to combat. They represented every branch of the U.S military—everyone and everything that happened in the war zones of Iraq, Afghanistan, and Kuwait. It was my privilege to serve as the Gateway Chaplain, helping them along their way and listening to their stories.

There was a pattern to each day that I have often described as the waves of an ocean going in and out. One could walk into a briefing tent and find it empty and quiet, but in just a few moments it could be packed with service members on their way home or back to war. Once I understood this movement I could position myself to be at the right place and time to be with them.

This is a representation of such a day, compiled from contacts and events during my deployment. The stories are woven into a narrative that allows you to spend a 24-hour day with me as I encounter the amazing members of our American military. The stories of the service members are compilations so as to protect the anonymity of individual soldiers. My story, however, is real, as I struggle with being God's agent in a harsh and distant land, trying to help meet the needs of our brave men and women in the military.

I wrote this book for the many of us who are trying to understand and help service members going through a deployment in a war zone, to help us understand why it is difficult to come back, and why such an experience is forever implanted in our mind and our very being.

If we can understand we can listen,
If we will listen we can hear,
If we will hear,
We can be God's agent for healing and peace.

0100—Welcome Back!

—ˠˠ—

Greet one another with a holy kiss.
All the saints send their greetings.
—2 Corinthians 13:12 NIV

"Welcome back!" I exclaim as I thrust my hand forward to shake hands with two rows of fast-moving military personnel arriving back from the U.S. The Atlanta plane was late tonight and the group of nearly two hundred is filing into the briefing room at 1 a.m. They are here for a few short briefings; one of them will be from me, the Gateway Chaplain.

I am met by looks of exhaustion that I can easily understand. The men and women have traveled for many hours—perhaps days—as they left their homes in the U.S., traveled to Atlanta to catch the chartered jet, flew to Kuwait, and then were bused to our base. Those who are deployed for more than a year, primarily Army, are given the opportunity to return home for 15 to 18 days through the Rest and Recuperation (R&R) leave program. The R&R is usually midway into their 12-to 15-month deployment. Now these Soldiers are on the last part of the return trip; here they will be divided up and sent to their particular locations in Iraq, Afghanistan, and Kuwait.

Most are bone weary, and some show painfully sad expressions after leaving their families again. They file by, accepting my greeting and doing their best to smile back at me as I greet them as warmly as I can.

Some are amazingly chipper, positive, and in good spirits. They're glad to be back in the uniform and back to what has become for them all too familiar.

Others are stone faced, perhaps mad or just too tired to express any feelings. They are merely going through the motions, following the person ahead of them.

"Welcome back; welcome back," I repeat as I shake hands with personnel in the continuous lines filing through the door.

"Ah, ma'am," a Soldier groans. "How can you say that? That's almost an insult."

I smile at him and say, "You know, Soldier, I've thought about this a lot, and do you know what I came up with?"

"What's that, ma'am?" he returns.

"Welcome back!" I say with a smile and a chuckle as I gently pat his shoulder while he continues to move past me.

I *had* thought about it quite a lot, agonized over it, prayed about it. I was told I would do this return briefing before I went to my new assignment somewhere in the desert of Kuwait. My predecessor had established a routine, a battle rhythm if you will, that included daily greeting the service members as they left and then returned from their R&R leave.

The return trip to Iraq can be dangerous for service members who have just been home. Sometimes the jolt of the transition is too much to take, and two chaplains are stationed here to help them. Every night one of us does this late-night briefing and invites them to visit with us if they are having trouble. We then wait, and they come.

One of my first late-night counseling sessions was with a troubled young father. He had just left his wife and toddler son. When he first came to the war zone nine months earlier, his son was a baby. Now on his return, his son was a bubbly little boy, full of need for his daddy. It was obvious he had fallen deeply in love with this little boy, who was now old enough to respond to him. I could imagine the two of them wrestling on the living room floor to the sound of giggles or the little fellow atop his daddy's shoulders as they walked through the mall.

The young dad was sitting in my office shortly after the briefings, crying profusely. He came to see me not so much to express how upset he was about leaving his family but more in panicked horror at the emotional outburst he was having and could not control. Soldiers don't cry, at least not when they're with other Soldiers. He was so panicked about the emotion that he could not sort out what he was emotional about.

As a woman, I couldn't help but think, *Well this is all very normal, good even, and of course you are upset and crying.* But it was *not* "normal" to him. It seemed he had never before felt such deep emotion. The haunting thought of never seeing his little boy again lingered just below the surface, veiled by the panic. It was tearing his heart out, and mine was a close second.

I tried to convince him that his feelings were normal, but he continued to look at me with terror in his eyes. He was afraid he would lose control and cry in front of someone, or horror of horrors, lose control at a critical moment in the war zone. I understand. In a place where disciplined control can mean the difference between life and death, emotional control *is* important.

I snapped off another tissue, placed it in his hand, and prayed that God would give me wisdom and the right words to help him. I talked with him, trying to convince him that the emotions he was feeling would come and go, but they need not overwhelm or frighten him. As it often does when I counsel with someone, an image came to me that I shared with him. I likened the welling up of his emotion to the first time one learns to ride a bicycle. I said, "Maybe someone gave you a push down a hill and you wobbled your way along when you first began. It was scary, wasn't it? Maybe it took your breath away, as you struggled to stay up on the moving bike. You felt out of control. Eventually the bike stopped rolling. You just had to hold on and find your balance.

"Your emotions will be like that," I continued. "They feel scary, wobbly, out of control, like you are going to crash. Eventually you were able to ride the bike without fear, and a time will come when the emotions you feel will not overwhelm you. You will find your balance and ride the emotion, and the emotion will not ride you. Just hold on and ride it. It will stop," I told him. "Just hold on; it *will* stop." I then encouraged him to seek more help if he needed it.

Not long after that another story that affected me greatly came from yet another young dad returning from his R&R. He showed me a picture of himself with his wife and baby. "We had this made while I was home," he told me, proudly holding the picture out for me to see. "I'm so glad we had this made because we may not…" His voice trailed off, and we both knew exactly what he meant. *We may not have another chance to take a family picture* was what he could not finish. Obviously he had seen enough death to know that he might not make it back to see his baby nor for the baby to know him as his dad; only this picture would remain.

Shortly after this was Father's Day. In filed the long lines of Soldiers, Marines, and select others. As I stood in the doorway shaking hand after hand, I felt apologetic. I gasped at the awesomeness and privilege of what I was doing. Looking into face after face after face, I was haunted by the fact that on average, three military members per day were being killed that month, June 2007. I also knew that 126 service members, most of them Army, were killed in action the month before.[1] Would one of the faces I looked into this night belong to the next person killed in action? Undoubtedly some of those would not survive another trip home. Some of those hands would never shake anyone's hand again. My breath shortened, and I had to step out of line as my lungs squeezed in an asthmatic response to this realization.

When it came time for me to stand before the group, all I could see were the faces of fathers sitting in the audience; lovely men between the ages of 18 and 60 who left their children and grandchildren on Father's Day to return to a war zone. I stood before them and could barely speak because I was so emotional. I said something to the effect that I was sad they had to spend Father's Day traveling back to the war, leaving their children behind. My voice cracked, and I almost cried in front of this crowd. My hand shook as I held the microphone. I recovered as best I could and finished my talk, but the crowd had taken on my mood. They looked broken and sad.

I took this mood to the throne of heaven for guidance. *Oh, God, this cannot be. What can I do? What should I say? Why am I here?* I cried out in prayer. God spoke to me clearly, not so much in words or in a momentary flash, but clearly. He said, *You are my eyes, my hands; reach out and touch them, look into their eyes and share love and concern. I love these Soldiers; tell them this.*

I determined to do just that. I would give each service member all the energy I could possibly muster, receive from God, and accept from the many prayers of those who were praying for me. I would, with great intention, shake each hand, look into their eyes, and greet them as they passed by me. My commitment to this small task became powerfully driven. I would pass on to them the divine energy of faith,

---

[1] http://icasualties.org/oif/

hope, and love, and I would pray fervently for their protection until they returned home again.

****

Welcome Back

"Welcome back," I say with a smile.
"Welcome back," though I know all the while
Of the agony, the pain, the hurt, the disdain;
Of the danger, the anger, the cunning stranger
Who lurks in the darkness intending to kill.

"Welcome back," I say with determination
Yet all the while I feel the consternation
Of worry, hurry, a flurry of tasks
To do before the next one asks,
"Can you help me?" and I pray my fears are still.

"Welcome back," I say again
For I hope to guide them to stay within
The borders of faith, hope, and love,
The borders of protection, affection, not rejection
Of the love of God and His mighty zeal.

0200—Marines!

—〰—

He (Jesus) took the five loaves and the two fish, and looking up to heaven, He blessed and broke and gave the loaves to the disciples; and the disciples gave to the multitudes. So they all ate and were filled.
—Matthew 14:19-20 NKJV

And whoever gives one of these little ones only a cup of cold water in the name of a disciple, assuredly, I say to you, he shall by no means lose his reward.
—Matthew 10:42 KJV

Turning the corner into another briefing area, I find the room full of Marines.

Oh, fun! is my first thought. *A group of Marines going home!* They were full of life, enthusiastic and…hungry. Marines always seem to be hungry. This is a fun fix for me because our supporters from the States send candy and goodies to be handed out, and a boxful came in the day before.

The favorite on a hot day was freezer pops. A hot and tired Marine, just arriving from Iraq, came up to me one day and asked, "Ma'am, can you tell me where I can get some water." My heart melted as I looked at him. He looked so weary. "Sure," I said and proceeded to tell him where the water cooler was. He had been sent out to gather water for his group. "Hold on," I said and hurried to get him a big hand

17

full of the frozen pops from my small office refrigerator. As I handed him the treats, his eyes widened with delight. "Score!" he exclaimed with a huge smile, as if I'd just given him the keys to a new Trans Am. It may have made his day, but it sure made mine!

I come back into the briefing area with the retrieved bag full of candy and snacks. I start out down the middle aisle. As I reach in the bag, I pull out a small candy bar, and hold it up. Hands instantly go up in the area, and I toss it across the aisles into the waiting grasp of a smiling young Marine. Another retrieval and toss, and soon it becomes a game. I take a handful of the candies and toss them across the crowd. Candy bars are intercepted by the guys in the rows ahead, and a howl lets out as if a football pass at the Super Bowl had been intercepted by the opposing team.

"Ma'am, ma'am, over here!" they beg, and a handful goes their way. The athletic and playful Marines jump from their seats to intercept the flying treats, laughing as they win the prize and pompously display their catch before gobbling it down.

"OK. Are you ready?" I warn, so as not to hit anyone. I gently toss another handful up and over and it rains down into the crowd. Not much to worry about with this group; not a piece is missed. I'm having a blast, laughing at the fun they are having with this little distraction. Cameras flash, capturing some of the excitement. It feels like Mardi Gras; for a gal from Louisiana, this is great fun.

One morning not long ago, I had walked into the same briefing area, and another group of Marines were there. They had started their day at 3 a.m., packing up their equipment, clearing out of their area, and loading on buses for the ride to the Gateway. By the time they got here it was still early morning, but in the busyness of the morning some of them had missed breakfast, and others were ready to eat again. Unfortunately, they had to sit and wait through several briefings before they could move out to their next destination where there was food.

I walked slowly down the aisle in the middle of the seated crowd, taking a visual inventory. A quietly spoken and drawled out "hel-p" came from somewhere near me. I looked down to find a young Marine sitting obediently and timidly in his seat.

"Are you OK, Marine?" I asked.

"I'm so hungry," he whined in such a pitiful voice that I have to chuckle.

"You pullin' on the chaplain's heartstrings, Marine?" the gruff voice of his first sergeant boomed. I continued to laugh as they sorted through whether it was OK to ask a lieutenant colonel for food.

"Ma'am," the young Marine continued, "if we had just one little Fig Newton." He drawls in a thick Appalachian twang and then gestures the rest of his sad story. "We'd cut it in half and share it between us."

"Ooohhhh myyy," I laugh out the words and then erupt in giggles. He definitely has hooked me and reeled me in. "I can fix this," I insist and disappear for a few seconds to return with a couple of chocolate chip muffins. The two Marines are delighted and wolf down the muffins as quickly as I had retrieved them. The Marines around them are looking on, and I can't help but want to feed them all.

"Sergeant, if you will loan me two Marines, I will get you enough muffins for the whole group. It won't be much, but it will tide you over till you get out of here."

He calls out three young men, and we began a trek across the base to a food storage area. After explaining the situation to the NCO there, we are given three boxes with 100 muffins in each box. The Marines took the boxes and walked them back to the briefing tent where they ripped open the boxes and tossed the muffins out to the waiting Marines.

For the rest of the day, Marines came up to me and said, "Thanks for the muffins, ma'am."

"You're welcome," I'd say with a smile. "Thank you, for what you do. "

It is indeed a joy and privilege to help them in this small way.

****

In 2004 a wounded Marine receiving treatment at Landstuhl Regional Medical Center (LRMC) in Germany shared with me his desires to get well and go back to Iraq as soon as possible to be with his buddies. I can't say that I totally understand these feelings, but it is a very common attitude. It inspired the following poem.

I'd Rather Be There Than Here

It's hot and dry
Got sand in my eye
But I'd rather be there than here

The food is lousy and never enough
We drink warm water from a thin metal cup
But I'd rather be there than here

Farmer by day, insurgent by night
Why don't you come on out and fight!
Just when I thought that I could sit down
In comes another mortar round!
But I'd rather be there than here.

There's nothing to say that hasn't been said
Watched all the movies and the books are all read
Bored out of my mind and scared but won't whine

Cause I'm a Marine and I'm doing my time

And I'd rather be there than here.

0300—Soldier

—ᴍ—

Wait on the LORD; Be of good courage,
And He shall strengthen your heart;
Wait, I say, on the LORD!
—Psalm 27:14 NKJV

My home in Georgia has a long, deep back porch on which sit two white rocking chairs. I made sure my real estate agent understood that a porch was a necessity. We were both delighted when she found my "perfect" house. From the porch I look through white columns, past the yard with the roses that my husband and I planted, onto an uncultivated green hill leading to a lovely patch of woods. Beautiful tall trees sway in the breeze, while chattering birds go about their work. Occasionally we see a Red-tailed Hawk or deer, and the sound of a rushing brook sings to us after a hard rain.

Here in Kuwait, rain was something I had not seen for months. Even when it did finally rain in the late months of winter, it was not more than a hard sprinkle. I dreamed of the hard rains in Georgia, as I sat on my back porch rocking in the white wooden rocking chair, enjoying the cool mist and the incredible cleanness of the air, the aerial display of lightning that erupted across the sky, and the thrill of anticipating the thunder clasp that would come next.

My Georgia home was large enough to accommodate an office where I could work. My duty as an Army Reserve

Chaplain entailed some work every day to keep up with the task of ministering to Army Reserve troops. Because of a painful shortage of chaplains in the Army Reserves, my area of responsibility covered three states and over a thousand Soldiers, plus their families. My "weekend warrior" status pays me for two days a month; the rest of the hours I do as a matter of conscience.

As I sat at my desk one afternoon, the phone rang. "Rachel, we need you to go to Kuwait. Their chaplain backed out at the last moment, and there's no one else to cover." It was the Regional Readiness Command Chaplain's office calling. The voice on the phone was a fellow reservist activated for just such duty as he was now fulfilling, making this call. A kind and gentle man, I trusted him to have my best interest in mind. I knew he would not match me with a job that was beyond my ability.

"Who are they?" I asked, a bit in shock.

"They're a unit composed of both active duty and reservists. I'll give you the contact number of the chaplain, and you can talk with him."

"OK," I answer as I hurriedly scratch out notes of our conversation.

"Rachel, they need you in two weeks."

"Two weeks!" I gasped. At the time my husband, an active duty Air Force chaplain was in Baghdad, Iraq. This meant that I would have to prepare legal custody for my son to live with someone else while we were both away. It meant I would have to close the house, find someone to watch it, stop the mail, set up automatic payment for bills, make arrangements for my cats, get my gear together, and pack for a year away. My mind whirled, and my stomach sank.

"Call the Fort Bragg chaplain. He'll advise you. You can do this, Rachel; we believe in you," my chaplain friend advised before hanging up.

Stunned, I took a stenographer's notebook, went to the rocking chair on the back porch, and began to write out my to-do list as it came to me. Head spinning, I closed my eyes to pray and rest in the assurance that God would get me through this.

"Ma'am." A voice startles me out of the memory of my back porch in Georgia. It is 3 a.m., and I am waiting to see if anyone from the Atlanta R&R flight will come in for counsel. Sometimes the R&R is so wonderful that it is agonizing to return, but for some the time at home is terribly disappointing. Either can spell disaster to a service member, one who is about to be re-issued their weapon and sent back to the war.

"Come in," I say to the young man and point out the chair set up for counselees next to my desk.

"My wife told me to come in," he began. He looks like he is just out of high school, too young to be married, separated, and carrying the stress of war on his arching shoulders. But the fact that he is married does not surprise me; many of the young Soldiers are married and have several children.

I roll my chair over to be closer to him and pause a moment as I take stock of his countenance. He sits slumped over, looking down; he is so quiet that he would be easily overlooked in a crowd. His small frame is overwhelmed by the large chair. He sits quietly, with his head down, wondering what he should say next.

"Why did your wife want you to come in?" I ask to jump-start the conversation.

"She is worried about me," he manages to say. If she is worried, I am worried. I listen intently while he continues. "I called her from the airport and told her I was having a really hard time coming back here."

I imagine many things that this could mean, but I wait and let him tell me more.

"I'm afraid, ma'am. Afraid I might hurt myself." The sentences are coming slowly. I listen patiently; keenly aware of the potential danger this young man is in. There have been a number of suicides downrange; one of my jobs is to intervene before this happens.

"I tried to cut my wrist, but all I had was a small disposable razor. I pulled the blade out, but it wasn't big enough to cut very deep. His long-sleeved uniform covers his arms, and I don't ask to see what he has done.

"When that didn't work," he continues, "I took all the pills I had. I didn't have very many, so it didn't work either." There is a pause, and I breathe in deeply as I take in the sadness of this story.

"I'm scared," he says with labored breaks between each phrase. "I'm afraid I'll try it again."

Even before now, I know what will happen. I will walk him down to the medical clinic; a doctor will evaluate him and confirm his need for help. The doctor will contact mental health at the larger base nearby, and the young man will be transported there for further evaluation. If they affirm that he is indeed in danger, he will be sent for further evaluation and treatment.

As I gently talk him into going with me to see the doctor, I know the situation will be out of my hands soon. I could stop this conversation at any time and get this process rolling, but I have bonded with this young man. He seems so sad and lost and so in need of someone to just listen. So for an hour we sit there and talk, and he tells me his story.

****

He Waits

He stands in humble silence, and waits for my permission,
To invite him in to sit a spell, to quiet myself and listen.

I wait for him to tell me, what this is all about.
He waits to see me listening, before he will let it out.
I wait to hear his story, before there's an answer to seek.
He waits to see if I'm hearing, then he begins to weep.

It washes us down a spiraling hole,
spinning and twirling and falling.
It washes us down a spiraling hole,
where the darkness is appalling.

We wait on God to speak to us, to hear His counsel wise.
We wait to hear God speak to us, to see it through His eyes.
God waits till we are listening, before He gives direction.
He waits till we can see Him, His help is our selection.

He waits for he is frightened; he waits for he is scared.
He waits and I wait with him, and God waits in sacred still.

0400—Troop Medical Clinic

—〰—

For behold, He who forms mountains, and creates the wind,
who declares to man what his thought is, and makes the
morning darkness, who treads the high places
of the earth—
the LORD God of hosts is His name.
—Amos 4:13 NKJV

We have been talking for close to an hour, and it is clear the young man needs more professional help. I explained to him the procedure of going to the TMC (Troop Medical Clinic) and the further evaluations he would go through. I have grown close to this young man and want to see this thing through. I suggest it is time to walk to the TMC; he agrees.

We walk out into the late-night air to find it refreshingly cool. After the intense heat of the day, it had taken until after midnight for the air to finally cool down. Soldiers are waiting in the courtyard to stage for their flights back to Iraq or Afghanistan. They have made themselves comfortable by lying on the ground, using pieces of their gear as pillows.

I find it amazing how Soldiers can sleep on the piercing rocks that cover the compound. In fact, I am amazed at how they can sleep almost anywhere. I have a collection of pictures of Soldiers asleep in the most unusual places: sitting up atop a stack of soft drinks; hanging backwards through a set of bleachers, using one step as a pillow while feet dangle from the other; and sleeping on the rocks under large shades while endlessly waiting for the next movement. But the most common sleeping position was on the desert camouflage baggage that matches their uniforms. Lying among the bags and using them as pillows, the Soldiers blend in so well that you can hardly see them. I call this the "Where's Waldo?" picture.

We walk to the TMC, around and through sleeping Soldiers and onto a dark road that leads to our destination. The pungent smell of the latrines has become so common that I hardly notice anymore, but the smell wafting from the row of trailers that house the toilets is especially strong tonight. I tuck my head and cover my mouth and nose to avoid the smell until we pass.

The moon is a delightful full yellow, beaming its light through the shadows of the tents to our sides and illuminating the gravel road. "Oh, look how beautiful the moon is," I croon, but he can't hear my words over the incessant blast of the generators pumping life into the lifeless desert.

A song that my husband and I used to sing together spoke of being separated by long distances yet always under the same moon. As I watch the glowing orb above the young Soldier and me, I think of my husband and son. They moved to Arizona without me, and my husband started his new job as wing chaplain at Luke Air Force Base, without the support of his wife. They packed up our belongings, stored my beloved rocking chairs, mothballed my lovely home in Georgia, and moved to a small house on a base that I have never seen. It leaves me with a strange void; how can one be homesick when home is a place I have never seen? I would not see my Georgia house again for quite some time.

I miss my family terribly but push the thought down and press on in order to cope with the challenges of this deployment. As I walk along the road, my wounded warrior in tow,

I take a side trip to be with my husband and silently sing our song as we walk

Arriving at our destination, I stop on the porch to again explain what will happen. The young man nods to acknowledge that he understands and then follows me in.

"Good morning, Chaplain," the Navy ensign sings out. He's a perky and bright young man who seems always to be in a good mood, and a bright smiling photo of him hangs on the wall to the side attesting to his competence, showing him as NCO of the quarter.

He takes a quick look my way; he sees the private with me and knows why I am here. We have gone through this routine before. Since I arrived here, I have walked someone down to the TMC almost every week. Most of them were in danger of committing suicide. This late-night visit could mean little else. The ensign, immediately alerted, responds appropriately and efficiently.

"We need to see the doctor," I say to him.

"Yes, ma'am. I'll get her." He picks up the telephone and notifies the staff officer on call. The nurse practitioner (NP), sleeping soundly in her pod across the street, is awakened and alerted to the situation. In just a few minutes she will be here.

My pod is just across the street also, and the lure of my bed calls out to me. But I have bonded with this young man and don't want to leave him. At this point, I feel as much like a mom to him as his chaplain. We sit in the waiting area and continue with small talk as we wait. He is anxious as he waits and looks sad and despondent, drawing me ever closer to my unofficially adopted son.

The NP arrives and sets up the exam room. She calls to him to go in, but he looks at me before moving. "Come on. I'll walk you in there," I say.

He sits on the examining table, and I stand beside him while we wait for her to come in. He looks so fragile and wounded that I can't help but put my arm around him as I speak words of encouragement to him. "It will be all right. They will help you," I say.

"We've got it now, Chaplain," a member of the medical team says to me, and with this, I am dismissed. Out the doors and onto the wooden porch of the small portable building that is the TMC, I find myself once again in the cool desert air. Down the steps and across the gravel street, I enter the area where I and the rest of the permanent party live.

I walk in the center of the carless road, remaining out of the shadows and watching the ground carefully, intending not to step on a scorpion. All of a sudden a shadowy figure moves behind me, and I jump and twirl in that direction, seeking out the culprit.

"Oh, Suzie, you scared me," I sound out. It is a desert fox my neighbors have named Suzie. About the size of a Miniature Pinscher, she frequents our area in the night, searching for food scraps. We rather enjoy her company and have adopted her as a friendly desert visitor.

Looking forward to the quietness of my room, I turn the corner and hear the shout of a familiar voice.

0500—National Guard

—⚏—

You lift me up to the wind and cause me to ride on it.
—Job 30:22 NKJV

"Hey, Mom!" I hear as I turn the corner, heading to my room. Outside my window, between the metal stairs and landings going into our rooms, a small sitting area had been built by the three young men who lived next door to me. They were from the Alabama National Guard, working as guarded escorts for supply convoys and for the buses transporting Soldiers.

We had developed a mother-son relationship. I gave them motherly counsel, and they helped me with little things and watched over me in a sweet, protective way. I often stopped and talked to them and listened to the many woes of their lives. At the top of the list were the females in their lives, followed closely by their supervisors and co-workers. They called me "mom," and I called them "son."

It was not uncommon to find my neighbors and a group of their friends gathered around the makeshift stoop at all hours of the night. Most of their work missions were at night, and they would stay awake until their 0600 PT (physical training) before going to sleep. This could cause a problem when I was trying to sleep, as the noise of the young people outside my window easily found its way into my room. After asking them several times to hold it down, I bought a small spray bottle to help me emphasize my exasperation.

Early one morning when the cackling crowd was loudly enjoying each other's company, I peeped out with the spray bottle of water in hand and squirted them. Jumping like a startled panther, one of the agile young Soldiers leaped from his chair, rushed up the three steps to the landing, and grabbed the spray bottle out of my hands before I could duck back into my room. Turning it on me, he doused me good, causing all of us to laugh. Our playful banter continued until they left.

By the time I got to the base, the Alabama National Guard unit had been there nine months, and going home was on their minds and a frequent topic of conversation. Finally, the day came when they were to leave. Like everyone else, they went through the arduous customs process. Eventually, they came to the last phase to the process, the outside formation area. They set up in a formation waiting to hear the last of the briefs before departing for the waiting buses.

I visited with them while they were in this last formation, and as time drew near the end, I made my way to the platform to tell them goodbye. I offered a prayer of protection over them as I did for others, only this time it was much more personal. Here was a group I had become very fond of, and I held dear their playful and protective nature. As I fought back tears, I heard from the back of the formation a loud, "Bye, mom!"

"Bye, son," I said under my breath as I waved goodbye and shook a hundred or so hands belonging to members of the Alabama National Guard as they left for the United States.

Tonight as I turn the corner to my room, I wish for the call of "Hi, Mom." Instead, it is awkwardly quiet, just the glow of the moon on the aluminum siding and a quiet sadness in my heart.

"You'll miss us when we're gone," I remember Jessie saying...and I did.

****

Several of the guys were very good musicians. They often played their guitars and wrote songs in the smoke shack. The lyrical country sounds brought out the country in me, and I penned a country song to croon out my feelings about my separation from my husband.

> The wind is blowing hard
> Hard upon my door
> Calling, calling to me.
> Come and ride with me
> Come and find reprieve
> Let me blow you, blow you away.
>
> My mind it wonders far
> While holding this guitar
> Blow me, blow me away.
> Sailing in the breeze
> Flying above the trees
> I'm blowing, blowing away.
>
> How did this begin?
> How will this thing end?
> Blowin', blowin' away.
> It's taken me so far
> Far from the one I love
> Blow then, blow me back home.

Come and take me home
Home where I belong
Blow me, blow me away.
Pick me up today
And send me far away
Blow me, blow me away.

0600—My Life in a Pod

—ᴖ—

She is not afraid of snow for her household, For all her household is clothed with scarlet. She makes tapestry for herself; Her clothing is fine linen and purple.
—Proverb 31:21-22 NKJV

"I live across the street in a pod," I sometimes explained to a service member with whom I was talking. "I guess that makes me a *padre*," I finish with a grin, hoping to get a little chuckle from the listener. Sometimes they got it and sometimes not, but this didn't deter my zeal for a good pun. I was often on the lookout for good wordplay to lighten the day.

Yes, I lived in what they called a "pod." I don't know where the term came from; as far as I know it was just the odd name for the buildings we lived in. They were prefab buildings partitioned off with eight rooms on one side and eight on the other. The buildings sat off the ground on cinder blocks, and a three-step metal stairway with a three-foot landing was outside each door. On windy days I would hang on to the door till the last minute, hoping I would not get blown off the landing. I never did, but several others told tales of tumbling off the steps on blustery days.

The room size was by my estimate about 12 by 15. A typical room housed three persons, holding three beds, three clothes closets, sometimes three desks, and one refrigerator, not to mention personal items. Residents partitioned off their area with sheets hung from the ceiling so each person could have some privacy.

The female latrine was in a small trailer about a hundred yards away from my room. A female icon was centered on the door to distinguish it from the male latrine. The female shower trailer was next to it, and a laundry trailer, filled with washers and dryers and a folding table, was next in this lineup.

My living quarters was high luxury compared to how some lived in Iraq and Afghanistan. It was humbling to hear someone come in from Iraq and be excited about how nice our facilities were. I remember one such experience at Landstuhl hospital during an earlier deployment. A wounded Marine lay bandaged from head to toe on his white-sheeted hospital bed. He said to me while I visited with him, "Wow, it's so nice here!" You learn not to complain or at least to be careful who you complain around; you just didn't know what others had been through.

While the typical pod held three service members, I had a pod to myself. The old adage that "rank has its privileges" applied here. As a lieutenant colonel I had a room all to myself, which meant among other things that I could decorate it as I wished.

My friend the nurse practitioner, also a higher-ranking officer, had a private room half the size of mine. She invited me into her pod one day, and I was dazzled by her clever decorating. A master shopper, she had taken full advantage of the base's weekly bazaar to collect treasures from Kashmir, India, Pakistan, and other exotic places.

"Oh, my goodness!" I exclaimed as I turned around in her small room, taking in the lovely decor. I felt as if I had walked into a sultan's palace. Lining the walls and on the bed were beautiful blue bedspreads, each a little different but in matching colors and coordinating patterns. On the floor was a beautiful blue woven tapestry, and draped from the ceiling over her bed she had fashioned a canopy with a sparkling matching scarf. The sparkly scarves from Pakistan would become an obsession of mine. I enjoyed buying them, gave them as gifts to transient guests, and sent them to friends and supporters.

"Oh, I love this!" I gasped out with childlike enthusiasm. "How did you do this? Will you help me do my room?"

"Sure," she responded with similar enthusiasm.

Thursday came, with the little bazaar forming a semicircle in the recreational area of our camp. I was there early looking for coordinating bedspreads. I chose spreads with a deep red background and lovely embroidered gold patterns in the foreground. With the bedspread came matching pillowcases that I filled with pillows or used as table coverings. I bought a beautiful red silk serape like Indian women wear, and after trying and failing to figure out how they wear this long piece of fabric, I draped it over my single captain's bed as a canopy.

Borrowing my friend's industrial stapler, I stapled the bedspreads to the walls. A stuffed white tiger, who growls when you press his left paw, was the finishing touch to this decorating frenzy. My little pod had become a palace. It was a wonderful retreat from the trauma around me, and I was glad to finally be home, with a chance to sleep and dream.

****

Now I can tell you how my day began. It started early this morning with a briefing to a large group going home for R&R.

0700—Gateway Chaplain

—ιυ—

*For a shepherd comes through the gate. The gatekeeper
opens the gate for him, and the sheep hear his voice and
come to him; and he calls his own sheep by name and leads
them out. He walks ahead of them; and they follow him,
for they recognize his voice.*
— John 10:2-5 TLB

"**G**ood morning, everyone!" I shout out over the microphone. A resounding "Hooah!" comes back to me from the large group of Soldiers gathered in the first of several briefing tents. This 7 a.m. briefing begins what will be a long day of briefings and security checks that proceed their two weeks of R&R. The process can be frustrating, and the young Army reservists who work this area have been the recipients of that frustration from weary and stressed travelers. My brief introduction to the troops involves asking them to be patient with the staff and to let them know our chaplain team is here to support them.

"Is this your day to go home?" I shout to stir their enthusiasm. Again, they energetically shout "Hooah!" back to me.

"Wonderful!" I pronounce, and we all enjoy a second of gleeful joy.

"I'm Chaplain Coggins, and I'm the Gateway Chaplain. You are now passing through our Gateway."

I loved the title "Gateway Chaplain." Early during my tour here, a fellow chaplain preached about Jesus as the good shepherd. He shared the illustration of a shepherd standing at the gate and watching carefully and intentionally as the sheep pass. "The shepherd," the Air Force Reserve chaplain said, "is looking for the wounded, the hurt, and the lame, the one who needs healing ointment and caring attention."

This illustration touched me deeply. I could sense God speaking to me as the chaplain gave this illustration. *This is what I want you to do. Look for the spiritually wounded, the hurt, and the lame, and administer healing. Take my healing ointment and apply it.*

At the outset, I was told I would be doing "Band-Aid" ministry. This image implied there was little I could do of any real consequence here, because the troops come through and leave so quickly. This image suggested that the best I could do was stick a metaphoric Band-Aid on the hurts and send the Soldiers on their way. My ministry vision became much deeper and more profound after I heard "The Good Shepherd" sermon. I now know that what I am doing here is administering God's holy ointment to wounded souls. I know that this ointment is powerful and miraculous, far beyond our limited comprehension and far more medicinal than a Band-Aid.

In the physical realm, a small wound can heal well if the proper medication is applied soon enough. This same wound, however, can become infected and even cause death if the infection continues unchecked. In the same way a soul wound can heal when God's healing ointment is applied. It can prevent and heal deep spiritual and emotional trauma.

I adopted this metaphor to explain what I do as the Gateway Chaplain. I stand at the gate and watch as the sheep go by. I offer healing ointment in the form of words, prayers, handshakes, or just a passing connection. It may seem like a little thing, but a little can be much when God's anointing is there. I consider it a great privilege and a holy calling to be the administrator of God's healing balm.

Continuing my brief introduction, I say, "If there is any way we can help you today, please let us know." I then tell them how to contact our chaplain team of two chaplains and two assistants. Just before I hand the microphone back to the teenaged Minnesota Army reservist giving the briefing, I offer one more word of advice. "Let me warn you, this is going to be a long day. So let me encourage you to make a friend, be a friend, tell a story, listen to a story, and enjoy your day today. Tomorrow you will be home. Hooah!"

"Hooah!" they blast out in one voice.

****

A sweet old spiritual comes to mind when I think of a healing ointment. The Old Testament word that is used and written about in Jeremiah is *balm* and it is melodically described in this song.

There is a balm in Gilead
To make the wounded whole;
There is a balm in Gilead
To heal the sin-sick soul.

0800—Emergency Leave

—⁓⁓—

How long must I wrestle with my thoughts and every day
have sorrow in my heart.
—Psalm 13:2 NIV

The Scheduled Airlines Ticket Office (SATO) opens at 0800 each morning. Military members on emergency leave (EMLV) arrive 24 hours a day and go out quickly. Those who have come in during the night file into the SATO office to arrange their flights home. It is one of three main places EMLVs will be today, and I will go to each location in order to minister to them.

Inside the SATO office I position myself to greet the exhausted EMLV who have arrived here late the night before. I am here to listen, to care, to guide, to help in any way I can. Five Soldiers, two Marines and an Air Force officer appear, and I speak to them collectively.

"I'm Chaplain Coggins. The chaplain's office is in the next building. We have a nice sitting area, coffee is on, and we have a phone you can use to call back to the States. If you need one, we have phone cards. The chaplain assistant is there now and can help you. We also have a clothes closet if you need civilian clothes. Just let us know what you need; we're here for you."

"Thank you, ma'am," they say collectively. Another group is coming in, and I repeat the introduction.

A service member is sent home on emergency leave for three primary reasons; the death of a parent, spouse, or child; extreme illness of a parent, spouse, or child when and if their visit will have a significant impact; and the loss of the caregiver of their child. An average of 29 emergency leave military personnel come through here each and every day.

I look over the 15 who are waiting in the SATO office to see how they are doing. It is painful to see them. Some of the reasons for going home are anticipated deaths; others are a great shock. Most of their stories are just plain sad, but some are tragic beyond description. Many stir up old feelings they have buried so deeply they forget they are there.

Sitting in the far corner, a young Marine waits to be called forward to schedule his flight home. His father-in-law has died, and his wife is terribly upset about losing her father. He is no stranger to death. He has lived with it since this war started. He has learned to block it from his thinking, but the death of his father-in-law has caused a flood of memories.

Three years earlier while in Afghanistan, his best friend was blown apart in front of him while they were engaged in a firefight. As he sits quietly in the SATO office, he sees it all again, like a movie playing in the foreground, blaring loudly and distracting him from the task at hand. The images invade his mind, invade his peace, and invade his very being.

He wants to take the distracting video and smash it to pieces so he will never see it again—only the video player is his mind, and the "off" button is broken. He rubs his head, a gesture that emphasizes the pain that is there, and wonders if he is losing his mind.

I go over and quietly sit next to him until he is called forward. Without words, I let him know I understand and hope and pray for his healing.

****

A Marine's Story

Deep in the open jaws by night
We arouse the sleeping Anger.
Flashes of light on gnarled teeth
Reveal the imminent danger.

It bites down hard and holds me tight
Rage throws me into the fight.
My heart responds with a forceful flood
Thrusting adrenalin and hot blood.

I fire my weapon with skillful hands
One down, then two, others will follow.
I taste the taste of life and death
And respond with controlled wrath.

Cries from Pain distract my concentration.
I turn and see a lighted trail
Invade his bulky body.

The flashing bullets – slow
The deafening noise – fades
The nauseating smell – remains.

The horror I witnessed I'm blank to describe.
It ended his existence, yet forever resides
– in my mind
– in my being
– in my dreams.

How I wish that I could change it.
– the propelling missile
– the misplaced Marine
– the horrible consuming scene.

How I wish that I could sleep.

Yet –

Inside the steel clasped jaw I remain
Consumed by the scene that reminds me
Of the sight, of the sound, of the smell, of the taste
Of the battle that swallowed my friend.

0900—Next Stop Iraq

—๛—

The LORD is good to those who wait for Him, to the soul
who seeks Him. It is good that one should hope and wait
quietly for the salvation of the LORD. It is good for a man
to bear the yoke in his youth. Let him sit alone and keep
silent, because God has laid it on him.
—Lamentations 3:25-28 NKJV

Stepping out of the SATO office, I stand perched on the platform of a metal stairway about three feet high that leads to the office. This spot is for some reason one of the highest spots on the camp, and from it I can see much of the camp and surrounding area. I often stop and look out and enjoy the view, watching planes go by and thinking of the adventures or struggles these travelers will encounter.

Today an army unit is staged in an open area next to where I'm standing. They have been at a nearby camp receiving the last of their training and were bused here for further movement. They will be here for a very short time and then will be on to their duty station in Iraq. Of all the groups who come through our area, they receive the least amount of attention from me.

They stand in formation, always in formation. Even when they are not told to stand in formation, it just naturally happens. Four long, straight lines of weary, hungry Soldiers. They are loaded down with an obscene amount of equipment—body armor, Kevlar, goggles, very large and heavy assault packs on their backs, and a large duffle bag at their side. But the thing I notice the most is how very quietly they stand. Not a word, not a sound, not a murmur of any kind comes from the group. They stand in silence awaiting instruction.

I stand quietly too, wondering what I can do for them. I've tried to speak to such a group before, but the smiles and well wishes that I give to those going home are inappropriate for this group. I marvel at the fluidity of the job with which I am tasked. Just a few steps away is a group ecstatic about going home, ready to receive smiles and a word of joy, a silly joke, but not this group. They are going to the most dangerous place in the world, and some of them likely will not be returning. They are silent and waiting.

The silence is broken by a young lieutenant who has stealthily made his way over to me.

"Ma'am," he says almost in a hush, "do you know where we are and why are we here?"

I sigh sympathetically at his question, but at the same time I am a bit amused. I keep the amusement part to myself. I understand his confusion. They were roused well before dawn, got their gear together, and were then bused here from the training camp. In the predawn hours they had little or no knowledge of where they were being driven; they're just following what they are told to do.

"Yes, Lieutenant, I know where you are and why you are here." I motion for him to join me on the landing of the steps, and from the pinnacle I point out where he is, where he will go, and why he is here.

"Will we have a chance to eat? We haven't had break-fast." My mother's heart is stirred, as I can hardly stand to see them hungry. It is not my place to dismiss the group, but I have enough rank to send them to chow, and I weigh the possibility.

"Do you see the golden arches down there?" I point out the McDonald's. (Yes, we have a McDonald's on our post, and it is enormously popular. Even when there is wonderful free food in the dining facility, the lines are longest at McDonald's.) I point out the other options for food and am about to suggest to the Lieutenant that he assemble a detail to watch the bags and send the rest down to find food.

Just then a sergeant, with information about their movement, positions himself on a barrier and begins to shout out instructions. "Listen up!" he begins and then proceeds to tell them where they need to be and when. My lieutenant friend has joined the crowd circling around the sergeant to hear the instructions.

I stand there long enough to hear him give instructions for finding food, and then I move on, satisfied that they will eat before they leave here.

****

Lord, be with these Soldiers. Help them to find comfort. Comfort in a restful spot, a warm meal, faithful support from home, and in the camaraderie of each other. Lord, they will not find the best of these things apart from you. Most of all may they find you, O God. May they find you.

1000 — The Hero

—〰—

When David was told, "Uriah did not go home,"
he asked him,
"Haven't you just come from a distance?
Why didn't you go home?"
—2 Samuel 11:10 NIV

Walking quickly back to my office area, I slow down to take a look at the Soldiers sitting along the wall waiting to talk to a liaison representative. An officer with the seasoned look of a battle-savvy warrior sits waiting. His faraway look seems distressed but also peaceful, as one who has seen so many things that nothing much could faze him. He is deep in thought.

"How are you doing, Major?" I ask, as I slow down while passing him.

"Chaplain," he expresses heartily as he acknowledges the cross above my name tag. "You got a minute?"

I sit beside him, and he begins to talk in an easy unhindered way, as if we had talked together many times in the past. This is not unusual; there exists a great trust between service members and chaplains, and often they talk with me freely.

"My wife wants me to get out of the Army," he says. It appears he wants a female perspective on this, as he continues to tell the story. "We have been separated more than we have been together in our eight years of marriage. The last three years we have hardly seen each other. She's just getting tired of it."

"Yes, I guess so," I empathize.

"But I'm good at what I do. I'm really good at it." He leans forward and with growing passion begins to tell of some of his adventures. "You know, I was one of the first Army Rangers in this country. We retook the airbase after Saddam Hussein had taken over."

He continues to tell me stories, and as he talks my mind weaves together the images that he describes. The movie playing in my head is a blockbuster account of the battles and engagements he has been through. A handsome and vigorous young movie star is dashing about exotic places all over the world, with bombs, missiles, and machine guns firing, and screams for help sounding in the background.

Having never been in a battle myself, I rely on Hollywood to fill in the blanks as I try to understand what the Soldiers are telling me. *Black Hawk Down, Saving Private Ryan, Blood Diamond*, perhaps even a toned down *Rambo* appear in my mind's eye as he describes rappelling into metaphorical snake pits and extracting high-value targets.

I sit back and listen in the same way one would sit back during a big-screen production and drink in the story that he tells me. His voice begins to slow and he comes back to where he began. "I'm good at what I do, but my wife says if I don't come home she'll leave me."

"Wow," is the best I can come up with as I allow myself a moment to readjust my eyes from the darkness of the movie theater.

I'm not a stranger to these stories. Landstuhl Regional Medical Center in Germany was filled with stories of heroism. Time and again I was asked by hospital visitors to take them to that special patient who had the hero's story. Often this person was not on the ward but standing or sitting against a wall patiently waiting in line or unassumingly walking the hall on their way to another appointment. Some of the most unpretentious people can be the most heroic and are often passed up by those looking for the bigger-than-life hero.

The major I am talking to, however, fits the bill of a Hollywood hero. Looking like a dashing young Robert Redford, the Special Forces Soldier is clearly in a dilemma. Which will it be—his job or his wife and children?

"Can I tell a story now?" I ask.

"Sure, go for it, Chaplain." He sits back ready to listen.

And so I begin my story, a story I have put much thought into and have told many times to show that the difficulty of going home from the battlefield is nothing new. Hopefully this helps people better understand this phenomenon and helps them with their choices.

"There is a story in the Bible about a man named Uriah, who had a very beautiful wife named Bathsheba. Uriah was described as one of the Army's 'mighty men,' perhaps our equivalent of an elite Special Forces Soldier. At the time of this story, he was away from home at war.

"One day while he was gone, his wife was outside on the roof of her house bathing. Now, this was not unusual. In those days there was no indoor plumbing, and they washed in the rain containers on the roof. But on this day it just so happened that the king, King David, was out on his balcony trying to pace away his boredom. He looked down and laid eyes on the beautiful Bathsheba and was completely smitten. The king had his servants bring her to him, and to make a long story short, she ended up pregnant.

"Now David is in a dilemma. Uriah is one of his best Soldiers and one of his most faithful men; offending him will be tragic. When Bathsheba is found to be pregnant while her husband was away, she will be stoned to death— not to mention how this will look for David, assuming Uriah doesn't kill him first. What should he do?

"What should he do; what should he do? Think, think," I gesture, tapping my forehead. "So David thinks up a ruse. He will pretend he needs information about the war. He will send for Uriah and have him return for a few days. He'll ask him a few questions and then send him home to sleep with his wife; hopefully, people would think that the baby was Uriah's and that it just came a little early.

"When Uriah arrived at the palace, King David greeted him courteously and asked how things were going."

"'Ahhh, yes, sir, king, sir,'" I playfully act out a nervous Uriah with a trembling salute, suggesting a person who is overwhelmed as he stands before the king. "'Everything is great, sir...ah, ah...king, sir.'

"'Good, good, glad to hear that, Uriah. How is Joab, the commanding general, doing?'"

"'Ah, great, sir; Joab is doing a wonderful job,'" I portray him saying, still holding the trembling salute.

"'Well, that's great, Uriah, thank you for bringing me this information. Now you've been working really hard and deserve a break; here's a little gift for your wife — go on home and enjoy some time off.' And David sat back to breathe a sigh of relief and commend himself on his cleverness.

"Now we would expect Uriah to cross the street and grab up his beautiful wife and...you know...but instead he is so consumed with his obligation to his men, his Soldiers on the battlefield, that he cannot bear to go home and enjoy his beautiful wife. Instead, he sleeps in the courtyard of the palace with the king's servants.

"When the king is told this, he is furious. He stomps up and down the palace hallway, pounding his fists in his hands and racking his mind for an idea. After calming down, he called Uriah to dine with him. 'Uriah, you need to relax.' David says. 'Here, enjoy this meal and my finest wine. Have some more wine, Uriah. Drink a little more, Uriah. Now go home.' David's intention is obvious.

"Still Uriah slept in the king's courtyard.

"David was *really* furious this time, and in his fury he wrote out a note for Joab the commander, telling him to put Uriah on the front lines in the next battle—and when the fighting was at its worst, to withdraw the men around him so Uriah would be killed. The king sealed the note and gave it to Uriah to take back to the battle with him. Within his pocket, the obedient Uriah took back to the commander his own death sentence."

"Wow, Chaplain, that's quite a story," the major finally gets to speak. He, like so many before, sat here absorbing this story and interpreting it in a variety of ways.

"Now, my advice for you," I said as I complete the story, "is go home, Uriah. Go home and love your wife, love your kids, make more babies. War will always be here; your family may not be." I left him there to ponder the story, and I go to attend to people in my office.

I pass him again a short time later, and he jumps up, hugs me, and kisses me on the cheek. "Thank you, Chaplain!" he loudly expressed with a huge smile.

Taken completely aback, I manage to mutter, "You're welcome."

****

Go home, Uriah, I say it so easily
As if doing so was a measly
Decision to be made.

Go home, Uriah, and yet I know
How difficult it is to stop and go.
Revision to be played.

Go home, Uriah, and love your kids and wife
Prayer and work will heal most strife,
Collisions will fade.

Go home, Uriah, work it out is my advice
Destruction of a family should not be the price.
Vision relayed.

1100—Walk to the DFAC

—〰—

Let your speech always be with grace, seasoned with salt,
that you may know how you ought to answer each one.
—Colossians 4:5-6 NKJV

"**H**i, ma'am, how you doing?" the smiling Navy reservist asks, adding the question to his salute. We are passing as I walk down the gravel road on my way to lunch at the dining facility, most commonly called the DFAC (pronounced dee-fak).

The ensign, like almost everyone who passes me each and every day, is rendering a military courtesy. Because I am an officer, he is supposed to acknowledge me with a salute. Adding the verbal greeting has become a common courtesy, and the friendly smile and genuineness of his question is typical of the courtesy and care that is exchanged among those of us who live on our small post.

A strong, positive response to the simple question "How you doing?" is expected. Not only is it expected, but it is something of a bragging right to proclaim that you are doing great no matter how difficult things are for you. It communicates that you are tough enough to take the harsh environment and situation, and you will Soldier on no matter what.

A host of colloquialisms have evolved to answer the question. Boisterously sounding off with "Living the dream, ma'am, living the dream," "It's another day in paradise," or an exuberant "Outstanding!" is always appropriate. Whining and complaining are never appropriate. The deployed military feed on each other's energy, and negativity is frowned upon and considered weak.

Our base is small, and this ensign knows I am the chaplain. He expects from me a positive response, an affirmation that today is a good day, a blessed day, and that I am not just saying this. He wants to be encouraged that someone *really is* having a great day in this seemingly forsaken place. And he expects from me the truth, not a platitude. After all, I'm the chaplain and an officer, and I am expected to encourage, motivate, and offer a positive response.

This question—rather, the response that is expected of me—until recently had been a very troubling problem. I had begun to notice that I could not answer the question positively, much less enthusiastically. I was not doing fine. I was hurting. After months of listening to one traumatically sad story after another, with very little sleep at night, and difficult staff relations, I was worn to a frazzle. I missed the comforts of home, my friends, and my family. I missed my husband and son.

So when someone would ask me how I was doing, I could respond with a sedate "fine," but it was troubling me more and more. I would think, *How can I be fine in the middle of a war zone? And besides that, I don't feel well; I get blinding headaches; I'm tired; my joints hurt from walking on these rocks; and it is so hot, so excruciatingly hot. I'm miserable!*

But this young man who asked "How are you doing?" did not deserve a rampage. Nor did anyone else. They had also left their family, the ones who care about them; they left their jobs and life at home. They deserved a kind answer and an encouraging word. Isn't that what chaplains do? Encourage people. Doesn't Scripture say, "I can do all things through Christ who strengthens me"? Doesn't it say, "Love bears *all* things" and "Hope *never* fails"?

But I was failing. I could not detach from the sadness of the stories that were being poured out on me. It was an enormous challenge to go from listening to a disaster to smiling enthusiastically to a colleague. Like passing through streetlights. Stop, go. Empathy, enthusiasm. Sad, happy.

It was this mental banter that sent me to the nurse practitioner on base. She was more than simply one of the two primary caregivers on our base; she was also my friend. So as I sat on the large inflated exercise ball that added to the clutter of her office, I wept out my dilemma.

"I'm having a really hard time," I cried, head down, hiding my face behind my hands. My head hurt with blinding pressure; I wanted to throw up, and I was too weak to stand. My body was acting out what my mind could not assimilate. If it weren't for the outdoor latrines I may not have made it out of my room that morning. But I *had* made it out, and I stood heaving over the toilet for far too long. I wanted to lock the door and not come out.

This was the second time this had happened, and it scared me. Was this physical, stress-related, or emotional? I could not sort it out. The physical pain, accompanied by the haunting voices in my head calling me weak and incompetent, was like the clapper in a warning bell floating on a stormy sea. Clang! Clang! Clang! The pain tossed me back and forth with spiteful vigor.

"I hear all these sad stories and they are so upsetting to me," I whined, "and then I walk out and people speak to me"...I trail off.

"They want you to say everything is fine, don't they?" she finished for me.

"Yes," I moan with a hint of enthusiasm, so glad she understood enough to finish the sentence. "I can hardly do it," I add.

In the blink of an eye, she completely switched the mood of the moment. "Let's get your hormones checked," she chirped cheerfully. I was 53, and it was no secret that I was in the middle of "the change." But instead of being with people who knew me and could understand the mood swings, hot flashes, and pain, I was with a revolving group of young people who expected an example of steady leadership.

She turned to her computer and typed out the arrangements to have blood work done while giving me instructions on where I should go and what I should do. "In the meantime, why don't we try a mild antidepressant?" she asked.

Silence permeated the tiny room as I pondered what she had just asked me. I had wondered if I needed a little help. Depression has been a part of my life; it was never really serious or incapacitating, but at times a haunting nemesis, hiding in my personal closets. How much of this is normal and how much should be managed medically are difficult questions to answer. I had talked with a doctor about it before, and he thought I was fine. Now, here was a medical professional asking me if I wanted help to get me through menopause. Or was it this deployment?

"Why not," I announced after the silent pause, and we discussed my options. A few weeks later after the blood work was done, I went to the neighboring larger base and met with a women's health professional. After a long talk and a review of options, he wrote out a prescription for hormones.

Something must have worked, because I was in a much better mood and had more control over my emotions. So, as the young ensign passes me on this drab, torturously hot morning and asks, "How you doing, ma'am?" I proclaim enthusiastically, "Wonderful. Thank you. How are you doing?"

"Great, ma'am," he responds.

"Fantastic!" I exclaim. "Have a great day."

"Thank you. You, too, ma'am."

1200—Seasoned Lunch

—ɷ—

The glory of young men is their strength;
of old men, their experience.
—Proverbs 20:29 TLB

He adjusts his hearing aid and leans forward to hear our conversation over the noise. The dining facility is packed with military personnel from all branches, plus international troops. They are busily moving about, finding the hot food, the sandwich or salad bar, looking for that special drink, and then finding a seat in the crowded facility. Lunchtime is the busiest of all the meals. The R&R Soldiers going home will start their briefings soon, a process that will take them the rest of the day. They are getting a good hot meal before beginning the long customs process. The full-time staff and other travelers are all taking time for lunch in one of the best DFACs in theater.

The Vietnam veteran I am sitting with volunteered to come back to active duty after the 9/11 attack on America. At first they told him no, that his hearing impairment would eliminate him from going. Now, however, he sits across the table from me and shares some of his story.

"Yes, I'm going home to see my wife, my two kids, and my four grandchildren. My wife has been a good sport about this. She's been very supportive. I miss her and my kids, but I sure do miss my grandkids. It will be great to see them."

He tells me this with a slight mist in his eye, but he distracts himself with the meal before him.

There are a number of us out here in uniform who are old enough to be grandparents. We're not the majority, but we are here. We are in good health and strong enough mentally and physically to take on this challenge.

"Chaplain, I have a story to tell you," he starts again. "It is my best chaplain story. Once when I was in Vietnam we were trapped on a hill, and most of my company was dead; only a few of us were left. A helicopter came, and out jumped two chaplains, one Protestant and one Catholic. They were coming out there where we were in the midst of this danger, to be with us, encourage us, and pray for us. We loved seeing them come; even though it was dangerous, it was a great boost to our morale to see them out there."

I am very proud of our chaplaincy heritage, and I consider it a great honor and privilege to serve as an Army chaplain. The Chaplain's Corps has been a part of the American military from the beginning. Our role is enormously important. Those who want to separate out religious support for the military criticize what we do and how we do it, but I believe that even for those who will not accept it, God's covering expands, and everyone is blessed by the ministry and the fervent prayers of the chaplains.

"Well," my lunch companion continues with his story, "The priest was in a bright-colored vestment that was a sure target for enemy rounds. I told him this wasn't good; he needed to leave that off. The priest told me he had to wear it. I told my mother about this, and she took camouflage material and made a vestment for him to wear."

I enjoyed the story from my new friend, the Vietnam vet. It's a reminder of how many things have changed so drastically in the military and how many of these changes some of us have seen. Plus, it's encouraging to see someone older than me out here.

Periodically things will happen to remind me of just what a large age difference there is between me and the young military around me. One day I said something about my deployment during the first Gulf War. The young private I was talking with perked up and said, "Ma'am, I was in kindergarten when that war started." At that time some of our Soldiers weren't even born yet, and some of the young people who are on battlefields today were in elementary school when the attacks on September 11, 2001 happened.

Yesterday I went over to talk with an attractive young woman. She was sitting on the floor, leaning against her duffle bags with her hands propping up her face. She looked so sad that I was concerned and went over to speak to her.

"How are you doing?" I asked.

"Oh, I'm fine, Chaplain. I just miss my grandchildren."

****

Grandma's on the Battlefield

Don't worry, daughter; don't worry, son,
Cause grandma's time has come.
We're out of the nursery, out of the kitchen,
Out on the battlefield mending and fixin.'

They say elite forces are much to be feared,
But the one to worry about doesn't grow a beard.
Peering through the sights and lookin' over the dash,
Is a red-hot-momma havin' a hot flash!

This image may cause you to stop and pause,
If you haven't thought of a lady during menopause,
Carrying a weapon and heavy flak vest
Donning ACUs, Kevlar, the whole mess.

We're driving the trucks and shootin' the guns
We're patching up the Soldiers, our very own sons.
We're pullin' guard duty and dying too
'Cause we're not left behind; we're right beside you.

So look out insurgents, we're comin' in
And we're stayin' till you play nice again.
O my goodness, golly gee
Grandma ain't what it used to be.

1300—Storms

———∿∿∿———

*So I said, "Oh, that I had wings like a dove! I would fly
away and be at rest. Indeed, I would wander far off,
and remain in the wilderness. I would hasten my escape
from the windy storm and tempest."*
—Psalm 55:6-8 NKJV

The walk back from the DFAC was horrible. A dust storm
was at its height, and walking through it I was pelted by
the blowing sand and debris. It was like a blinding snow-
storm but with sand and very hot wind. The wind pushed
against me so hard it was difficult to walk forward. Holding
a tissue over my mouth and nose with one hand and hanging
on to my headgear with the other, I staggered along the
quarter-mile walk. With my large sunglasses protecting me,
I squinch my eyes closed, barely able to see a thing. There
was no need to see, though; I had done this walk enough to
do it without looking.

I could get pretty spun up about the dust, especially in
our office. Our office was a sectioned-off area in a large
constructed tent with a concrete floor. The tent was an oblong
structure with canvas covering the large steel beams that
arched from one side to the other. When the wind blew, the
tent would flap and snap with a loud popping sound. When
this happened, our large tent would turn into what I called
a noisy playground. I called it that because the squeaking

frame of the tent sounded like swings on a playground. Eeeek, eek, eeek, eek. Besides the noise there was dust, always dust. There was dust on the chairs, on the desks, on the computer keyboard, on the floor. On dust storm days, it was really a mess.

The first few days after I arrived we had one of the worst dust storms. The noise in the tent was so distracting and irksome I thought I would go crazy. That, in addition to all the other new things I was adjusting to, was almost maddening. As time went by, I did get used to the noise, but I never did get over the dust. Each day we would arrive to a fresh powdering of dust all over everything. I must have complained about it more than I realized, because the chaplain assistant took offense. I asked him once to bring a dry mop from the chapel. He disappeared and came back with the mop. Throwing in on the floor, he yelled, "There, Chaplain Coggins! There's your mop!"

Good grief, I mused. *Where did that come from?*

People's emotions can so easily get out of balance, dealing with all the things that go along with a deployment. There are things I never did understand. I do know that being a woman in a predominantly man's world can make for some relationship challenges, but to be fair, it can be difficult for most everyone.

Relationships were by far the hardest part of this deployment for me. I had started out with 150 other reservists training at Fort Bragg, North Carolina. Much of the training was not relevant for me since I am a noncombatant (chaplains do not carry combat weapons or train with them), but I was told it would be important to develop relationships with the people I worked with. This never worked out. The first day I was in Kuwait, I was taken to a different duty station an hour and a half from the rest of the group and rarely saw them again. Even my chaplain assistant did not arrive until two weeks after I did. By the time he got here, I was adjusting to the heat, the noise, and the rhythm of the job, and he was in culture shock.

My first week in Kuwait I followed my predecessor around like a scared puppy on her first hunt. The heat and wind were abominable, and he trudged through it as if it was nothing. Talking while walking through the harsh elements, he passionately explained the ebb and flow of the operation here. It would take me weeks to figure out the ins and outs and comings and goings of the troop flow through the Gateway. When I finally understood the pattern, I could see the wisdom of the procedure the chaplain before me had put into place, where the positioning was best for ministry opportunities to the 1,400-plus military who flowed through the Gateway each day.

Explaining this to the new teams who came to work with me was not easy. Like me, their initial take on the procedure was that it was lunacy. They preferred to put signs up telling where the office was rather than visiting the emergency leave personnel directly. It was a war I would not win.

****

I wash the dust from my eyes and see
That all around me remains to be
Dusted, cleaned, shaken, arranged.
I feel strange, deranged, restrained.
How did I get here to this dusty place?
How do I continue with this task I face?
It will be later when I realize,
Yet another day before I surmise;
Some things cannot be fixed by dusting.
Some things cannot be fixed by fussing.
Some things just cannot be fixed.

1400—My Brother's Keeper

—∿∿—

How the mighty have fallen in the midst of the battle!
Jonathan was slain in your high places.
I am distressed for you, my brother.
—2 Samuel 1:25-26 NKJV

Military members on emergency leave are found sitting together in the back of the large briefing tent at this time of the day. They, along with the R&R passengers, sit here for about two hours while going through a series of briefings. I scan the back rows looking for anyone who might need to speak to a chaplain. As I look intently through the crowd, I pray for God's vision to lead me to find who needs help.

I have talked with several in this group during the morning, and they recognize me. Now they will have a chance to talk with me if they want. I notice a young man off to the side. He doesn't look upset, but something about his countenance alerts me, and I go over and ask if I can sit down.

"Sure," he says. "I'm fine, just sittin' here waitin'," he adds. The Soldier has seen the cross on my uniform and knows I am a chaplain and that I am sitting with him because he's on emergency leave.

"I'm escorting someone home," he volunteers. Soldiers are sometimes sent to escort the body of a fallen Soldier. It concerned me that they may not be emotionally prepared to face the family of the fallen Soldier, and I would talk with them about some things they might expect.

The other reason someone would be an escort was to accompany a fallen relative. I had seen them go out with a nephew, brother, fiancé, and a father taking home his son. These deaths are terribly hard on us all.

As I sit next to this brave young Soldier, caught emotionally somewhere between shock and denial, I ask him, "Is it a relative?"

"My twin brother," he announces matter-of-factly.

The answer is a blow to me, and I feel as if I have been sucker-punched. It takes my breath away, and energy drains from my body. I sit back hard, turning my gaze from him, and close my eyes for a moment.

"It's OK," he says to comfort me. "I'm fine."

But it wasn't OK. As I look at the athletically handsome young man next to me, I realize I see the exact image of a fallen Soldier, one who has just died for our country, for our freedoms, for me. I lean over, elbows on my knees, and I want to cry. I want to release teardrops large enough to puddle on the floor in front of me. I want to go outside and scream and wail. I do none of these things.

As I sit here, eyes closed, drinking this in, I begin to tear up, and as the drops trail down my cheeks, I take a tissue from the small pocket on the side of my pant leg, just above my boot where they remain ready. I offer one to him, and he says, "Nah, I'm good." "OK," I say. "I'll cry for both of us." I hope that my emotional expression will give him room and permission to find his feelings, but clearly I must deal with my own emotion.

I sit quietly for a few moments as the wave passes through me, and I regain my composure. My thoughts go to his mother, and I think to myself, *She will be devastated. She will probably have a really hard time letting this Soldier go back into the war after losing his brother and will likely try to talk him into resigning.*

"How's your mom?" I ask.

"Oh, she's plenty upset," he says and then goes on to confirm my suspicions. She had already let him know that she wants him to get out. The tabs on his uniform tell me that he is a serious Soldier, and at this point it is deeply ingrained into his being. He *is* an Army Ranger, and death is just a part of what he does. He is trained to suck it up and drive on. The game face doesn't come off even for this. I find myself a bit stunned by the dynamic.

I sit here a while longer and we talk about him, his family, his brother, and their relationship. Silently I pray for them all.

"Can I pray for you, Soldier?" To my surprise he agrees, and I place my hand on his forearm and pray a simple prayer of safety and blessing for his journey home. Then I move along.

Walking back to my office engulfed in a fog of emotion, I must look like one of the zombies from *Night of the Living Dead*. I pass one of the airmen from the base mayoral cell who asks me, "Going to the bingo game tonight, ma'am?"

"No," I murmur, lost in my emotional daze, while I think to myself, *Bingo? We play bingo here?*

****

I cannot say what confirms my feelings of sadness, anger, and crying out for help better than David does in Psalm 55. A Soldier, a commander, and a king, he understands a warrior's pain.

Listen to my prayer, O God. Do not ignore my cry for help!
Please listen and answer me, for I am overwhelmed
by my troubles.

My enemies shout at me, making loud and wicked threats.
They bring trouble on me, hunting me down in their anger.
My heart is in anguish.
The terror of death overpowers me.
Fear and trembling overwhelm me.
I can't stop shaking.
Oh, how I wish I had wings like a dove;
then I would fly away and rest!
I would fly far away to the quiet of the wilderness.
How quickly I would escape—far away from this
wild storm of hatred.
But I will call on God, and the LORD will rescue me.
Morning, noon, and night I plead aloud in my distress,
and the LORD hears my voice.
He rescues me and keeps me safe from the battle
waged against me,
even though many still oppose me.
Give your burdens to the LORD,
and he will take care of you.
He will not permit the godly to slip and fall.
—Psalm 1-8, 16-18, 22 (NLT)

1500 — Gold Star Mom

—ᶮᶷ—

Do not forget to entertain strangers, for by so doing some have unwittingly entertained angels.
—Hebrews 13:2 NKJV

B ack in my office I have almost an hour to touch base with my staff and go through email before heading over to Naval Customs, the last phase before military members go home for R&R.

An email from Debbie Lee reminds me of the awesome encounter I had with her and Melanie Morgan. Melanie — Mel, they call her — is a talk-show host and chairman of Move America Forward, an organization formed to support the troops.

Debbie is a Gold Star mom from Surprise, Arizona. Her son, Marc Alan Lee, was the first Navy SEAL killed in Iraq. He received the Silver Star for heroism after standing in the direct line of fire three times in order to cover his fellow SEALs while they evacuated a seriously wounded team member. He gave his life in order to save another.

Debbie joined Move America Forward and speaks around the country, thanking, honoring and supporting our troops. She has a contagious passion to help military members and their families, especially families who have also experienced loss. "They feel your heart," she says. "Who else can understand but one who has also experienced the same?"

The Move America Forward team spent a month driving from California to Washington, D.C., raising support for the military and getting signed cards of encouragement to give to the troops. Melanie, Debbie, Mary Pearson, and Danny Gonzales staged in Kuwait while on their way into Iraq to hand out the cards. They had accomplished an extraordinary feat; nothing about it was ordinary.

While the team was here, I ushered them into the briefing room where over 300 Soldiers and Marines had just been briefed on what they could and could not take through the customs area. The troops were waiting for the next phase of this process, which gave us an opportune time to speak to them.

I took up the microphone as I did most days and began to address the group. "Are you ready to go home?" I shouted out with enthusiasm.

"Hooah!" they shouted back.

"Hi, everyone. I'm Chaplain Coggins, and I have some special guests I'd like to introduce to you. These lovely ladies are traveling though our area on their way to Iraq. They have a very special mission, and I'm going to let them tell you what they are doing."

I handed the microphone to Melanie, and she eloquently introduced herself and the others, telling everyone of their mission to bring 226,000 signed cards to troops. An engaging speaker, she was not remiss in telling the military personnel how much they were appreciated and how she and her organization, Move America Forward, stood behind them.

After she spoke, an amazing thing happened. A Marine walked up to Melanie and said, "Ma'am, you say you're from the San Francisco area? Do you know Mrs. Diane Layfield? She is the mother of my friend Travis, who was killed in Iraq."

With a stunned look on her face Melanie answered, "Yes. I know her." Melanie and Debbie work with a support group that assists family members of KIA military, and this woman is one of the group.

"Ma'am," the Marine continued. "Will you do something for me?"

"Of course, what is it?" she answered.

He took a brass bracelet off his arm and extended it toward her. "I've worn this bracelet in Iraq in honor of Travis, and I'd like his mother to have it."

Engraved brass bracelets commemorating a personal friend are often seen on the arms of military members. Impressed on the bracelets are a fallen warrior's name, rank, and the date they were killed. I have also seen tattoos honoring a lost friend. Remembering their friends in a special way is extremely important.

Melanie took the bracelet and promised to give it to the young man's mother. As I listened in the background, I shook my head in amazement, thinking *Only God...*

After Melanie spoke, Debbie took the microphone and blinked in awe as she found herself standing before the large crowd of uniformed troops that had just left the war zone. To her, they collectively represented her son Marc, who had given his life. Her passion as she stood before the troops was palpable.

"This is the most difficult crowd I have ever stood before," she said. Her voice cracked, and she was for a moment overcome with emotion.

"My son, Marc Alan Lee, was the first Navy SEAL killed in Iraq," she told them. "I, as much as anyone, know the great sacrifice you are making." I looked back to see the audience visibly moved. Easily stirred, many of them have lost friends, comrades, fellow Soldiers. They know the pain of losing someone, and here before them was a mother, embodying their pain and embracing it—a mother's heart open before them.

"I want to tell you 'thank you' from the bottom of my heart," her voice broke with emotion as she spoke with staggering staccato. "Thank you for what you are doing, and thank you for your sacrifices. We love you, and America loves you."

Debbie told me later that she normally speaks much longer, telling some of her son's story, but this time she was very brief, overcome by the emotion of standing before the large group of uniformed military. She handed off the microphone and turned around to gather cards to pass out.

Applause rose from the crowd, and from the middle, Soldiers began to stand. All over the room the troops stood up, and clapping thundered throughout the tent. It was an incredibly moving moment as the hardened troops, fresh off the battlefields of Iraq and Afghanistan, stood to applaud a mother from Arizona.

Debbie had to be prompted to notice the standing crowd. She turned and with a gasp partially covered her face. The applause of the crowd continued enthusiastically as she gathered the cards and began to pass them out.

$$************************$$

Some survive the death of their loved one and go on. Some are overcome by the tragedy and succumb to their own destruction. Debbie lost Marc in 2006. She chooses to help others survive and heal, and in so doing she also finds healing.

Don't tell me there is no hope when I just died for thee.
Just listen to my story…
And remember me.

1600 — Green Beans and Silent Means

—◊◊◊—

*Is anyone among you sick? Let him call for the elders
of the church, and let them pray over him, anointing him
with oil in the name of the Lord.
And the prayer of faith will save the sick,
and the Lord will raise him up.*
—James 5:14-15 ASV

The last phase of the customs process takes place in a
waiting area on the far side of the camp. Within the
fenced-in compound are several large tents filled with chairs,
a courtyard for formations, and a few offices for the Navy
personnel who run this area. Today not only are the R&R
Soldiers here, but a Marine unit, two Army units, and an Air
Force unit are also waiting to go home after completing their
tour in the war zone. It is great place for me to interact with
the service members before they go home, and I will spend
the next three hours here talking with them, helping them
when I can, and in general being available.

Great, I'm early, I think. *I have time to indulge in one of
my favorite things, an afternoon cappuccino.* The line outside
the small trailer that is the Green Beans Coffee Shop extends
down a metal stairway into their small outdoor seating area,
which is shaded with camouflage netting. I join the line and
engage in conversation the people I am standing with.

"Hello, Mum," the worker says in thick Indian accent as soon as I enter the door. Seeing his big beautiful smile and contagious enthusiasm is one of the highlights of my day. He always seems to be happy to see me, and I am just as delighted to share our habitual brief exchange.

He and most of the workers on our base are subcontracted TCNs (Third Country Nationals). Most of them are from India, Pakistan, and the Philippines. I enjoy talking with them, but conversation is limited because of the language barrier. I have a good relationship with the ladies who clean our showers and work at the hair salon. Most of them leave home for two years at a time to earn money and send it back to support their family. It is a hard life, and stories such as theirs help keep me humble.

"Coffee mit pom," the Green Beans worker says as he sets out my cup. "Yes, coffee with foam," I translate with a chuckle as I take the cappuccino. "I'm covering this specialist and the private," I say as I point to the two young Soldiers behind me. I snap in the Eagle Cash Card to deduct the cost from my account.

"Thanks, ma'am, but you don't have to do that," one of the Soldiers says.

"Don't argue with me, son—I outrank you," I answer in playful banter.

"Yes, ma'am," they say with big smiles. Our conversation continues as we stir in sweetener and then go down the steps into the courtyard.

"Ma'am." The call draws my attention to a Marine sitting on an outdoor bench. Even thought he is sitting down I can tell he is more than six feet tall. He is a picture-perfect Marine—chiseled body, strong jaw line, perfect teeth, and a serious look that could win him a place on any recruiting poster.

"Were you at the Landstuhl hospital in 2004?" he continues.

"Yes, I was." I answer, looking closer to see if I recognize him. I do not, but I am instantly transported back to the hospital. An average of a thousand service members per month came through LRMC while I was there. They could come in bandaged, bruised, and bloody, and leave looking entirely different. I often would not recognize them a few days later, much less years later.

"I thought I recognized you. You prayed for me in the hospital," he finishes.

I am greatly humbled by the remark, so much so that I cannot comment. I try to think of a way to ask, *Which one were you?* but no way seems appropriate. A ring on his finger tells me he is married, and he seems very happy to be going home. It is enough to see him sitting there looking so healthy, strong, and handsome. It made my day.

People have said to me, "It's good that you pray with people; it encourages them." They miss the point. Prayer invokes the healing power of God when we are obedient to His direction. James 5:14-15 says, Is anyone among you sick? Let him call for the elders of the church, and let them pray over him, anointing him with oil in the name of the Lord. And the prayer of faith will save the sick, and the Lord will raise him up" (NKJV).

How awesome it is to be the agent of God and administer prayer to the willing.

****

Most of the time we do not know what effect our prayers have on others. This is one of my favorite poems that expresses this thought. I wrote it while I was at LRMC.

Silence

I walk into a silent room
And see a silent Soldier.
I stand in silence by his bed
And say a silent prayer.

Up stirs a sounding thunder
From deep within my soul.
I sense the voice of his mother
Pleading, oh my child, please hold!

Oh my baby, oh my son!
Where is he?
How is he?
What has been done?

I reach and touch his broken body
And pray divine healing will flow through my hand.
I feel it oh so strongly,
I falter there to stand.

I speak in words to the Father
With all the compassion of a mother.
Most Holy God I join the prayers
Of those who pray for him

You who knit together his body
Inside his mother's womb
Knit back this broken body
And send him home soon.

I turn and walk in silence
Out of the silent room.
What can be done in silence,
Will shout
throughout
Eternity.

1700 — Navy Corpsman

—⚋ᴧᴧᴠ⚋—

By this we know love, because He laid down His life for us.
And we also ought to lay down our lives for the brethren.
But whoever has this world's goods,
and sees his brother in need,
and shuts up his heart from him,
how does the love of God abide in him?
— 1 John 3:16-17 NKJV

"Going to South Carolina to see your wife and two kids?" I ask a National Guardsman as he passes me to get follow-on tickets for his R&R trip.

"Three kids," he says with huge smile.

I have made it a game to guess where people are going. I'm good at distinguishing accents, the ring on his finger tells me he's married, and it's a good guess that he has children. But the trick is identifying the patch on the left arm. Most everyone who's been around the Army knows the patches of the major units. I know many of them and quite a few of the Army Reserve and National Guard patches as well. If I don't know one, I'll ask and try to remember it for next time. The Soldier passing me at this time wears the renowned South Carolina National Guard patch. A fellow Southerner and citizen warrior, we both speak the language of friendly greetings.

"Oh, that's wonderful," I continue as he moves along. "You have a great trip home."

"Thank you, ma'am."

A Navy corpsman is next in line. Navy corpsmen are highly trained medics who accompany the Marines into battle. The story of a Navy corpsman is beautifully portrayed in the book and movie *Flags of our Fathers*. In it, James Bradley, the author, tells the story of his father as a young Navy corpsman in World War II. The movie starts out showing an aged man in fitful sleep, dreaming about his encounters with Marines on Iwo Jima. The scripted scene intercepts the dream and takes us to the bloody battle of Iwo Jima. All around us we hear the haunting cries of wounded Marines calling him, "Corpsman! Corpsman, over here! Help me!"

Flags of our Fathers shows us how deeply felt war trauma remains forever implanted in one's being. The movie shows how some overcome the trauma and some do not. While maintaining a successful life, this former corpsman continues to hear the cry for help in his dreams for the rest of his life.

My first heartfelt encounter with a corpsman came at Landstuhl hospital. Late one evening, I was visiting a patient in a four-person room. One of the bays held a wounded corpsman straight off a brutal battlefield in Iraq. We heard a commotion in the corpsman's bay as he and the nurse argued about how much pain medication he should have. The patient became very agitated, sprang from his bed, stormed down the hall, and headed outside. I followed, very concerned about his state of mind, afraid of what he might do.

Shadowing him down the hall without a word, I followed him through the empty corridor, down a stairwell, through another hallway, and then outside into a garden courtyard. It was dark, but the lights in the courtyard highlighted the benches, the trees, and the plants that had been lovingly placed to provide a respite for the wounded warriors.

The stars twinkled overhead and the coolness of the night air swirled through the surreal setting. Neither of us had yet spoken a word. There was nothing for me to say at this point; he would talk to me when he was ready. The young corpsman sucked down a cigarette, then another, and was on the third when he began to speak.

"They don't get it! They just don't get it!" he barked out. He went on to tell me stories about the Marines he had helped in Iraq. Some he helped save; some did not make it. He told me about opening the tailgate of a truck that held wounded Marines. There was so much blood on the floor of the truck that when he opened the tailgate, the blood poured out on him and soaked him through. It was days before he could get a clean uniform, so he labored on with the smell and feel of the Marines' blood on him.

He talked nonstop for over an hour, and then he just stopped and returned to his room. He had purged a great burden, but I was left with ingested images I can never erase.

My respect for these gentle warriors is enormous. This afternoon, as I stand beside the young man who continues to walk past me, I ask him, "How are you doing, Corpsman?" He looks forward, not engaging me, and with steeled determination he says, "I'm fine, ma'am."

I am disturbed by his response. His posturing, his eyes, everything about him tells me he is not fine. He's just giving me the standard answer, and there is no time to explore how he really is.

I reach out and gently touch him on the shoulder, "Have a blessed trip home, son."

"Thank you, ma'am," he says, not breaking his forward gaze, and continues on his way.

****

The Wounded Healer

The wounded healer sits alone
Upon the ideal he had made
And ponders all that came his way
And slowly starts to weep.

I cannot do this, I cannot sleep
I cannot hold these feelings so deep.
I have not finished, it is not complete
How can I go on with this feeling of defeat?

The wounded healer sits alone
Upon the ideal he has made
And ponders all that came his way
And slowly starts to weep.

1800—3rd Infantry Division

—ᒐᒑᒐ—

Have I not commanded you?
Be strong and of good courage;
do not be afraid, nor be dismayed, for the LORD
your God is with you wherever you go.
—Joshua 1:8-9 NKJV

Clink, clink, clink .... clink, the wind was blowing something against a tree, sounding a call for me to find the source. Someone had hung dog tags on a low branch of a young eastern redbud tree. Looking closer, I could see it was not a regular identification tag but had a U.S. flag background and an engraved prayer.

I held it between my fingers and read the familiar passage. "I will be strong and courageous. I will not be terrified or discouraged, for the LORD my God will be with me wherever I go." It is from Joshua 1:9 and is a popular verse of encouragement adopted by our Soldiers. Obviously, the Soldier who is remembered here wore these tags and probably had them on the day he was killed in Iraq.

I spent three days at Fort Stewart, Georgia, shortly before I deployed to Kuwait. I took the time to walk along the memorial sidewalk and was deeply moved by what I saw. A long line of redbud trees are planted between the road and sidewalk. I couldn't tell how long the row was, but I could barely see a young couple coming toward me, at the far end of the sidewalk. Still the trees continued past them, and a nearby field is filling with row upon row of the commemorative trees. These trees of honor each represent a fallen 3rd Infantry Division (3rd ID) Soldier. The trees that line the sidewalk form a memorial that was founded in May of 2003 to commemorate thirty-four fallen Soldiers who led the way into Baghdad when the war first began. At the time of my visit in March 2007 there were nearly 400 trees.

I strolled down the quiet sidewalk looking at the trees, the names of the Soldiers, and items left at the trees' bases by loved ones and friends. The names of the 3rd ID Soldiers are displayed at each base on a concrete marker within a small circular area surrounding each tree.

Some of the trees were bare but most had small personal items attached or placed in the rocks at the tree's base. A ceramic angel, a note, a flag, a picture all testify to a loved one's visit and lead you to imagine a tender moment when the article was placed there. I blinked back tears as I experienced the memorial to the fallen Soldiers.

Fort Stewart, home of the 3rd ID, is near Savannah, Georgia. Savannah is one of the oldest cities in the United States and one of my favorites. I helped the Georgia National Guard with an Army Marriage Enrichment Retreat there not long before I came to Kuwait. Giant live-oak trees adorned with long-hanging Spanish moss fill the courtyards and squares of the lovely southern city. They create quite a contrast to the small new redbud trees lining the road at Ft. Stewart.

As I continue visiting with the troops in the Naval Customs courtyard, I recognize the square patch with horizontal lines that distinguishes a 3rd ID Soldier and I hear the clacking of that dog tag against a redbud tree at Fort Stewart.

"How are you doing, Soldier?" I ask.

"Fine, ma'am," he says in a hush.

"How is it going up there?" I ask him.

"It's better than it was. It was rough for a while."

He's speaking of the surge and the deadly months of January through June of 2007. I imagine what he may have seen, not because I have a vivid imagination, but because the Soldiers sometimes tell me of their experiences. With these stories, the news reports, and the books by those who were there, I can weave together my own mental movie of what this young Soldier has just lived through.

His particular story may never be told. He, like many, will not win awards or be recognized for heroism, but in his humble way he will do his job, a job that most of us will not have to do because he does it for us—a dirty and brutal job that some don't seem to know exists.

This Soldier looks weary and worn, and I worry about him. Will he have nightmares; will he take out his aggression on his wife, on his child? Will he try to drown all he has seen by drinking too much? Will he do just fine and come back refreshed after reconnecting with his family?

Oh, Lord God, bless this young man and give him peace, I pray silently while we continue our verbal and nonverbal conversation.

"Will you go to Savannah while you're home?"

"Oh yeah, we'll make it into town," he says with a strained smile.

"I love Savannah; I hope you have a great trip home," I say.

"Thank you, ma'am."

"Thank you, Soldier."

****

Dude, We Are So Going to Die Today

"Dude, we are so going to die today,"
He'd say each day as we began patrol.
Facing his fear, pumping up to be bold
A little bit cocky, a little bit cold.

We're going to die today!
So face the ultimate fear.
Why be afraid, why be scared
When already our fate is seared.

"Dude, we are so going to die today!"
And with this comment, he walked away.
Into the dust, the dirt, the ash
Into the city, laden with trash.

Lurching near a buried IED
They pulled the trigger between him and me.
The horrific sound, the blinding flash,
Snapping bones and burning flesh.

Now I lie upon this bed
Wounded and fractured and bleeding.
I remember him saying,
"Dude, we are so going to die today."

And he did.

1900—The Road Home

—ᚹ—

Like apples of gold in settings of silver is a word spoken
in right circumstances.
—Proverbs 25:11 NASB

The early evening cool has brought the troops out of the large tents and into the courtyard. They are ordering pizza, smoking, getting coffee at Green Beans, and enjoying each other's company. A table sounds out from the hard slap of a domino as an enthusiastic player slams down his victorious play. It is accompanied by robust laughter. They are happy about going home and getting out of the battlefield, and excited about getting to see family and friends.

I meander through the courtyard and avoid an especially foul-mouthed Soldier. Generally just my presence causes most of them to clean up their language. This fellow has not seen me, and is much too engaged in his story to look beyond his small audience.

A Soldier walks up to me and says, "Chaplain, will you pray for me?"

"Sure, Soldier, what do you want me to pray for?"

"I want this trip home to be good for my wife and me. We need this time together to strengthen our marriage."

"Of course I can pray for that, Soldier," and with his permission I put my hand on this arm and begin to pray.

Other Soldiers come up and talk; some ask for advice, some just want to talk, but I'm looking for those whose hearts are troubled. I'm looking for that distressed Soldier who will carry way too much of this war home to his family. The transition is seldom easy, but in some cases it will be tragic. There are some who will be forever scarred by their experiences. I walk about hoping and praying that I can share a word or prayer, which when spoken at the right moment will make a difference in someone's life.

Soon it is time for the R&R to form the final formation. Two hundred troops assemble in eight long lines facing a wooden podium used by the briefers to give final instructions. While the key leaders are scurrying about to complete the process, I climb up on the podium to address the troops. There is no microphone, so I cup my hands around my mouth and shout out as loudly as I can. Slowly and deliberately, I shout my chosen words, turning my head to one side and then repeating in the other direction.

"Hello everyone, I'm Chaplain Coggins. I came over to tell you goodbye and to tell you I'll see you when you get back—Hooah!"

They respond with a less-than-enthusiastic "Hooah" as they acknowledge they must come back. Experience has taught me that many things can happen on the R&R trip home. I want them to know I will be here for them when they get back, and they can come talk with me.

"Please do come back," I continue, and they laugh. I say it as a joke, but we recognize that some will have trouble getting on the plane to come back. A very few will not come back, either because they go AWOL or encounter serious trouble while on leave. I am very concerned about them, and I try to express this concern in my brief comments.

"Let me be the last to remind you to please be patient. Be patient with yourself and patient with those around you," I shout from one side to the other. The transition from Iraq to the U.S. is mind-boggling, and as I point out a few of the stark changes, I hope to inject a little humor into this presentation to make it a bit more palatable.

"They have not been driving ... the way you have been driving." They laugh.

"They have not been thinking ... the way you've been thinking." They laugh again.

"And ... they have not been talking ... the way some of you have been talking." They laugh again, knowing I speak of the foul language that many of them pick up while deployed.

"So please be patient and make it a great trip home—Hooah!"

"Hooah!" they blast out.

"Now if you will allow me, I'd like to say a short prayer for you before you leave." The troops remove their headgear and bow their heads, eager to receive God's blessing. "Holy God, I pray that you will watch over them and keep them safe. May they have a blessed and wonderful trip home. Amen.

"Make it a blessed and safe trip home—you deserve it! Hooah!" I blast out while giving a thumbs up.

A loud, thunderous "Hooah!" explodes from the formation, and they smile and laugh with an almost giddy euphoria. It is the best moment of the day.

Soon the large group is ready to leave. I reach into my pocket and pull out a small bottle of anointing oil and rub it into my hands. A church in Ohio sent me the oil after each of the women of the church took turns holding the bottle of oil and praying for the troops. When I shake hands with them, the lovely scented oil will linger on their hands, as will the faithful prayers of the intercessors who pray for them.

The R&R Soldiers move out in single file, and I position myself along the walkway and shake hands with each and every one as they pass me. "Bye. Bye. Bye, God bless you."

I repeat over and over for half an hour while they pass swiftly toward the gate and are directed onto the waiting buses.

"Bye, Chaplain." "Thanks for the prayer." "See you when we get back," are some of their comments to me.

The last of the troops pass out the gate, and the bright day has changed to the night's sky. I wave goodbye to the gate guard and slip out the compound onto the gravel road leading to the DFAC. It's my favorite night at the DFAC, Surf and Turf night. I don't want to be late.

2000 — Bus Stop

—⟋⟍—

For now we see in a mirror, dimly,
but then face to face. Now I know in part,
but then I shall know just as I also am known.
— 1 Corinthians 13:12 NKJV

"**I**s it dangerous where you are?" I ask the attractive Native American woman as we walk back from the DFAC.

"No, ma'am" she responds pensively. "Just the snipers, the car bombs, the booby traps, the IEDs, and the VBIEDs" (pronounced vee-bids, Vehicular Borne IEDs).

"Good grief!" I gasp as I look on with amazement at the sturdy Soldier walking next to me. We had met over dinner, and as we walk back up the road she continues to tell me her story. She is the granddaughter of one of the Navajo Code Talkers whose heroic actions in World War II saved the lives of countless Americans. They used their rare Navajo language mixed with a code they had developed to transmit vital information over the airway. Their mix of language and code was never broken by enemy interceptors. Their amazing story is powerfully told in the movie *Wind Talkers*.

I am completely fascinated with this young lady and very impressed with her courage and will, but I must break off and go to the bus stop. The bus stop is the final place of the day where those who are on emergency leave will be found before the cycle begins again early in the morning.

"Chaplain, you might want to go see the guy sitting alone over there in the blue shirt," says my friend who manages the bus station. "He looks like he could use a word from you." She and three other workers are non-military civilian contractors. They are accustomed to my visits and help keep an eye out for distressed military members headed home on emergency leave.

"May I sit with you a minute?" I ask the blue-shirted young traveler. "Sure," he says, and he immediately begins to tell me his story. His father has died, and he's going home for the funeral. I listen patiently and ask him a few questions to help him tell me the story. He talks about his dad with great affection and tells me a few stories of their life together. I express my sympathy and ask if I can say a prayer for him. He gratefully accepts.

The room is filling up with a mix of military and civilians, about half going on R&R to places other than the United Stated, while the other half are on emergency leave. It is my goal to speak to as many of the emergency leave personnel as possible while they check in and wait for the bus taking them to the airport.

Sitting with earphones planted deep in his ears, a young man ignores everything around him. "How are you?" I ask him. "I'm fine, Chaplain," he says taking out one of the earpieces and looking up at me with glassy eyes.

"Do you mind if I sit with you?" I ask.

"Sure, go ahead," he says and makes room for me to sit. A brief conversation lets me know that his mother is expected to die, and the young Soldier hopes to make it home before she does.

"Have you thought about what you will say to her?" I ask.

"Just trying not to think about it," he says, which is the all-too-typical answer. Although these young Soldiers live with death all around them, the loss of a parent is something they are often unprepared to face. I talk with him about what to expect and suggest he think about what to say to his mom.

"This will be a very special moment that you will remember all your life. It is a precious chance to tell your mom what you need to tell her." He nods. "Maybe while you travel you could think about a time you and she shared that was really special to both of you and then remind her of this story."

"Humm, that's a good idea," he says. We talk a little more, and I say a prayer for him before moving along.

This scene repeats over and over as I make my way through the group that is continuing to gather. With each conversation, there is a strong sense of divine covering, enshrouding us in sacred seclusion—a holy moment between Chaplain and Soldier.

I use the metaphor of stepping into a telephone booth and helping the person to phone God. At this special moment of leaving a war zone to face a family tragedy, God is the one they need to talk with, and I help them make the connection.

I continue to move about the room, but as it happens far too often, I come upon a story that stops me in my tracks.

"My wife and son were in a car accident," he says. "They were hit by a drunk driver. My wife is in critical condition, and my son is dead." I surrender to a deep sigh and sit back; there are no quick words for such a tragedy.

"You know, Chaplain, you're over here because you think you are protecting your family from terrorists and people who would hurt them, and then something like this happens." He hangs his head shaking it from side to side. He heard this news two days ago and has been consumed with the images and thoughts his mind displays. It appears he has barely spoken since that time, and our chance encounter, or more accurately God-appointed encounter, provides an opportunity for him to express his deep pain.

"I'm afraid I'm going to have to hurt someone, Chaplain."

"What do you mean by that?" I ask the rhetorical question.

"Sometimes a man has to do what a man has to do."

It is my nightmare scenario. I will spend the next few moments before the bus leaves passionately reasoning with the hurting husband and father; hoping to convince him not to do what he has suggested. I end it with an equally passionate prayer and commend him to God for further care.

****

I look into a mirror and what do I see?
I look into a mirror and wonder what is to be?
I look through a mirror and know I will not understand
Until I get there, and ask You, while before You I stand.

2100—Covert Operations

—ɷ—

Hide me under the shadow of Your wings,
From the wicked who oppress me,
From my deadly enemies who surround me.
— Psalm 17:8-9 NKJV

I will trust in the covert of thy wings.
—Psalm 61:4 KJV

Two buses pull away from the bus stop while ten more pull in, demonstrating the constant movement that is the Gateway process. The big buses line up alongside the briefing tents, and out pour the Soldiers and Marines returning from their R&R leave. They are the first of two large groups that will come back tonight.

The troops file out and assemble in front of one of many signs that indicate to where they will return. Most will go to Iraq, others to Afghanistan and Kuwait. After instructions and a short break, they file into the in-processing area and officially check back into the war zone. Three long lines are squeezing through the door, and I begin the ritual that started before I came, one of greeting them with a handshake, a smile, and a warm "Welcome back." As soon as they are seated, we will start the briefing. I will give the first of three briefs.

My role at this briefing is to insure that they are stable and focused enough to go back to the war zone. No matter how much they miss their families, the troops need their focus to be on the dangerous job they are about to re-encounter. They need to stay focused to keep them safe, to keep them vigilant. If their focus is on problems at home, it can be dangerous for them and others. My aim in this briefing is to share with them courage and hope, spiced with a dash of humor.

"Welcome back. Did y'all have a good trip home?" I sound out using the microphone, accentuating my Southern accent. They respond with the familiar "Hooah," although it is not nearly as energetic as when they left here two weeks earlier.

I have found there are some typical things the military members do on their R&R. Some of these things are contradictory, and acknowledging this helps me point out that the R&R was great for some and not great for others. So, each night I begin by asking these three questions.

"How many of you got married while you were home?" Up shoot about a dozen hands. I count them off and then say, "Congratulations!" The crowd gives them a light applause, and many smile at the thought. A uniformed couple sits together in the far corner and both raise their hands. "Did you two marry each other?" I ask them. They nod yes. "Congratulations," I say. There are a few married couples serving together in the war zone. Sometimes they are allowed to live together, and sometimes they are not.

"Probably someone got a divorce?" This question shows the flip side of the honeymoon R&R. I don't really ask, not wanting to embarrass anyone, but a Marine, several male Soldiers and one female Soldier voluntarily lift their hands, while one enthusiastically shouts, "Yeah!"

This draws a chuckle from the crowd. I expect this response because it happens every night. I gesture and sigh, "Oh my, what's a chaplain to do?"

The third question deals with something I have become aware of during this job. Deployed expectant dads (pregnant female Soldiers do not deploy) plan their R&R to coincide with the birth of their child. So I ask, "How many of you had a baby or saw your baby for the first time? And grandchildren count!" All over the house hands go up. I see this every night, too, but the wonder of it never ceases to amaze me and the others. An organization called Adopt-a-Chaplain sent me Beanie Babies to give these expectant dads for their new babies. I called it "Project Beanie Daddy."

"Wow," I say to the new dads. "Keep your hand up." I begin to count. "One, two, three .....twenty-three, twenty-four! Twenty-four new babies! Wow! Let's give them applause." And a hearty hand clap goes out to the new dads.

"Y'all have been busy, I see." Everyone smirks and chuckles at the comment.

"Well," I continue. "Whether you had a great time with a honeymoon and new babies being born or a terrible time—and I know that some of you did—it can still be tough getting on that plane to come back here. Is that right?"

Throughout the seated group I see nods and hear murmurs of agreement.

"But whether you are glad, sad, or mad about coming back, the reality is—" I hold the microphone out toward them waiting for a response. The Army and civilian Gateway staff who work with me each night know this line, and as if it is a game, they lead off with the answer I want.

"You're back!" they shout out.

"Yes, that's it," I agree sympathetically. "You're back. And it's time to get your focus back. Because if you don't have your focus, you could get hurt: someone around you could get hurt. Is that right?" I again hold the mike their way, and they give a unanimous agreement, fully understanding the gravity of what I am saying.

"That's why I'm here. If there is any way I can help you, listen to you, help you sort out your feelings about what happened or didn't happen while you were home, so you can get your focus back, come see me, and we'll talk." I then tell them where to go and promise I will wait for at least two hours after this briefing.

I end my portion of the brief by saying, "Now for those of you who will allow me, I'd like to say a prayer of protections over you before you go back into theater." Most are very happy to have a prayer prayed over them and bow their heads to receive the prayer. I keep the prayer simple, short, and generic, expecting that those who understand will receive the prayer with the intention given.

Holy God, we join the prayers of many around the world
who are praying for their protection.
Hide them under the covert of thy wings, oh God,
under the shelter of your wings protect them,
and send them home safely again.
Amen.

****

The prayer I prayed each night was inspired by my childhood pastor in rural Louisiana. A portion of his prayer, inspired by the Psalmist, was this: "O God, hide us under the covert of thy wings." As a little girl I didn't know what *covert* meant, but it stuck in my mind all these years.

The term "covert operations" is a military term in which the sponsoring person is concealed but not the act. God does not hide from us, but for those who do not have eyes to see Him, he is covert, as is His protection over us. My constant, passionate prayer is that the powerful symbolic wings of God will hide Soldiers from harm and that they will come to know Him through the mighty miracle of God's covert protection.

I solicit your prayer that we can continue to speak these powerful prayers over the troops.

2200 — What I'm Fighting For

— ∿ —

Greater love has no one than this,
than to lay down one's life for his friends.
—John 15:13-14 NKJV

A basket sits at the front of our office with a pen and slips of paper close by to write out prayer requests. It is used often. I check the basket as I return from the briefing and find a prayer request that fills both sides of the small paper. I take it out and go to my desk to read it and pray.

The note is neatly printed in small block letters. A private from an infantry company stationed in Baghdad has asked for prayer for his fellow Soldiers who were killed during the surge. Twelve names are listed, both first and last names. I am intrigued with the note. I turn to the computer and log into a webpage on MilitaryCity.com, named Honor The fallen. This website lists every military service person who has been killed in action or died while in the war zones of Iraq, Afghanistan, and Kuwait.

Typing in the names of the Soldiers on the prayer request, I am able to find all of them. Most have a picture, a brief bio, and a newspaper article about the incident. I paste together the stories and the pictures and print them to commemorate the twelve fallen Soldiers.

They are a group of handsome young men, of varied ethnicity, most between the ages of 18 and 23; the oldest in the group is 31. I wonder about the young man who has written the prayer request. I assume he knew them well, because the names are lovingly written and spelled correctly, even though some were very difficult to spell. Soldiers can become very close to each other. Many of the young Soldiers, it seems, have few political or worldview idealisms; they fight for each other.

I sit here and contemplate the tragedy of losing twelve close friends, and a wave of sadness flows over me. I pray a silent prayer that only a grieving spirit can pray, and I know my Father hears me.

"Ma'am," the chaplain assistant says, "someone here to talk with you."

"Come on in," I say. "Just give me a second to finish this." The Soldier comes in and takes a seat. My office has no door or ceiling, but it is partitioned off in such a way that the person talking to me is completely blocked off from view.

I save the document I'm working on and roll my chair over to be close to him. I sit close enough to hear him so he won't have to talk in a loud voice. He doesn't have to say much to let me know what is going on. I know he is returning from R&R, and I know that way too often these trips home are disappointing, even tragic.

One look at him tells me we will need the tissue box that's on the two-drawer filing cabinet beside him. I place it within reach and snap off two tissues. One I give to him; one I hold for myself. He takes the tissue and immediately begins to weep into it. Experience, intuition, and the ring on his finger tell me the problem is most likely with his wife.

"She told me she wants a divorce," he says, beginning to get a grip on his emotions. "I'm losing the very thing I'm fighting for." His words have a powerful effect on me. This patriot believes in what he is doing, believes he is protecting America from further attacks, and believes he is creating a safer place for his wife and children. He is fighting for his family. Now the long separations are breaking apart the very thing for which he is fighting.

I will not have time to do marriage counseling. My primary concern is to help him survive the moment, and survive the deployment. I know how dangerous this is. The number one reason for suicide is the loss of a relationship. Here is a man losing his most important relationship, and we are sending him back to Iraq with a loaded weapon in his hand.

I speak gently and calmly and coax the story from him. We talk for over an hour, and he unravels the story that is knotted up in his mind, blinding him and hindering logical thinking. When it is laid out on the table, though, the problem is much more manageable.

After our talk and a long, heartfelt prayer, he leaves looking much better than when he came in. I, however, am exhausted. As the watch on my arm beeps 11 p.m., I sit back in my chair and close my eyes.

****

What I'm Fighting For

"I've lost what I was fighting for"
And his pain penetrates.
"I'm losing what I'm fighting for"
The painful statement resonates.
The Soldier who loses so much so dear,
We all lose with him and drink in his fear.
Yet we also share with him an unshakable spirit,
The strength and power of the collective unit.
And hence we've become,
An Army of One.

2300—Weep with Those Who Weep

—ᘐᘐ—

Rejoice with those who rejoice, and weep with those who weep. Be of the same mind toward one another. Do not set your mind on high things, but associate with the humble. Do not be wise in your own opinion.
—Romans 12:15-16 NKJV

The breeze was warm as it blew gently across the back porch of my Georgia home. Ceiling fans in the 15-foot ceiling cooled the warm wind while whirring a steady tune. The fan's pull chain clapped in rhythmic harmony. A rose-bush laden with lovely chartreuse roses added a fragrance to the grasses and trees that grow there. Birds sang and played in the tall trees near the woods down the hill. My large white wooden rocking chair held me close as we rode our way to a peaceful place.

My two cats loved it when I brought them outside to enjoy the fenced backyard. One lounged peacefully by, blinked at the bright sunshine, and collapsed on the cool concrete porch beside me; the other one dashed about chasing flying bugs and butterflies.

Two years earlier we were living on an island, stationed at Lajes Field in the Azores. The Azores are a Portuguese island chain an estimated 1,000 miles off the coast of Portugal. I'd been there about six months when the call came to mobilize and go to Landstuhl Regional Medical Center in Germany.

With barely enough time to say goodbye to the people who had become my friends, and parishioners, I was off to California to join an Army Reserve Medical Hospital. The 300 reservists bonded quickly and went to Fort Lewis near Seattle for another two weeks of processing. Then we were on our way to LRMC for nearly fourteen months. Before I was back with my husband and son, 15 months would pass. My son would change from a playful 11-year-old to a tall, deep-voiced 13-year-old before I could rejoin him.

Once again I am thinking of LRMC while sitting on my Georgia porch. I think about the many wounded Soldiers, Marines, and others that I saw, listened to, ministered to, and prayed with. On my lap lies a recently published book about Carrie McDonnall entitled *Facing Terror*.

Carrie tells the story of her call to ministry to the people of the Middle East. She began her work as a journeyman, a two-year program sponsored by the Southern Baptist Convention. I had applied for the journeyman program myself, and in much the same way as she had, I received my calling into ministry.

In Jordan, Carrie met the love of her life, David McDonnall. After they were married they went to Iraq with a team to help set up water purification wells in impoverished areas. On March 15, 2004, a delayed trip met with a fateful end; their pickup truck with five passengers was ambushed. Seriously wounded, she alone survived the ambush. Carrie was flown to LRMC where I worked.

I visited her late one night as she was lying completely sedated in an ICU room. The bond with my Baptist sister was strong. As I stood over her and prayed, I felt compelled to sing to her. I offered up an old Baptist hymn and then asked, as though she could hear me, "What would you like to hear?" A contemporary Christian song came to mind, and I sang the lovely tune, allowing its gentle and medicinal vibrations to fill the small room. I genuinely felt I was joining an angelic choir as we sang together for Carrie. I was moved to speechlessness when I read in the foreword to her book that she had heard singing while she was unconscious.

Many of the stories at Landstuhl would render me speechless. It was difficult to speak of the things I saw and heard, and I often sat in silence wishing I could write it out and heal myself from the tragic tales that trudged through my thoughts.

Poetry was my outlet while at LRMC. Many mornings when I got up I felt an overwhelming sense of sadness and began again to write poetry. The writing, which was a form of prayer, was a great outlet for the sadness and pain I was feeling. I titled the collection "We Cry Poems" after an idea a counselor gave me years earlier. He said I cried poems, and he was right. In my sadness, I would write poetry. It was certainly true at LRMC.

I sat on the cool back porch and reminisced while the cats continued their antics.

Meow. Meow! "Ma'am!" The voice finally brings me back from my slumber. I'm back at the Gateway. "There's someone here to see you," a sergeant smirks as he catches me napping in the chair.

"Oh, excuse me, I guess I dozed off." I stammer, embarrassed that I was napping.

I shake myself awake, stand to invite my visitor in, reach for the tissue box, and put it within reach of us both.

"I don't need that." His voice sounds gruff.

"It's for me," I answer, fully acknowledging what is about to happen.

I take a tissue for me and one for him and place it on his knee. He grabs it up and begins to weep.

2400—Epilogue: Time to Leave

—〰〰—

To everything there is a season, A time for every purpose
under heaven: A time to be born, And a time to die; A time
to plant, And a time to pluck what is planted; A time to
kill, And a time to heal; A time to break down, And a time
to build up; A time to weep, And a time to laugh; A time to
mourn, And a time to dance; A time to cast away stones,
And a time to gather stones; A time to embrace, And a time
to refrain from embracing; A time to gain, And a time
to lose; A time to keep, And a time to throw away;
A time to tear, And a time to sew; A time to keep silence,
And a time to speak; A time to love, And a time to hate;
A time of war, And a time of peace.
—Ecclesiastes 3:1-8 NKJV

When does compassion become compulsion? When does obligation become obsession? When does it get too personal? Had I crossed the line? How do you let go when there is a constant flow of need?

You'd think I would have been happy the day I was told I was going home. Ecstatic even. We all dream about the day we will be back with our families; the day we don't have to walk 100 yards to a latrine in the middle of the night, or find sunglasses before going to one in the daytime. But I wasn't happy. I started to cry. It began with delicate little tears escaping from the corners of my eyes and turned into uncontrollable wailing. I had to be taken to a private room because I was so upset. I cried and wailed into tissue after tissue, soaking half a box. Someone called my dear friend and former roommate to come over as quickly as she could. She dropped what she was doing and sprinted over. She was a perfect compassionate "chaplain" for this chaplain as she consoled me in my moment of despair.

I had seen this thing plenty of times at Landstuhl and again on this deployment. It's strangely painful to leave. I even gave it a name, "The Uriah Principle," which I have talked about in chapter 10. It wasn't about me; it wasn't about the job; it was about the emotional connection I had made with the military members who went through our Gateway.

I knew what it was, I had seen it plenty of times, and now it was happening to me. I was emotionally carried away, out of control, like someone caught by the torrent of a river. However, I wasn't afraid; I knew it would stop eventually. My quest would be to write out the story. Write until I could understand it. Write, and in so doing hope to explain to others why their Soldier has such difficulty adjusting to the homecoming.

There is a scene in the movie *Galaxy Quest* in which Tim Allen's character asks intergalactic aliens to help him find his shoes. In comedic fashion they look up and around, staring at the ceiling, totally unaware of what shoes are or where they might be found.

I sometimes feel it is impossible for other people to understand a Soldier's feelings. How can you know what shoes are if you have never seen or worn them? If a person has never worn boots into battle, can that person understand the drama, the passion, the obsession, the compulsion? How it takes over a Soldier's life and drives him or her? Drives him or her to think less and less of the other world they came from and focus more on the world that is now his or hers? Only it is all blurred. Blurred by the confusion, the fog of war, the obsession to stay alive and help the people nearby stay alive.

Someone said to me one day, "You think everything is a crisis!" I couldn't believe what I was hearing. I wanted to scream out: *What do you mean? Don't you see this? We're in a war! There is crisis everywhere. Can't you see how hurt these people are? How tired they are? How much their families are suffering because they have been separated so much?*

Was this reaction a symptom of over-intoxication of the pain and suffering around me and a sign of my need to step back and find healing? The questions continue to whirl in my mind, my spirit, my being. After going around in full circle, I end up back at the place where I started. Like the hands of a clock, with the chime in the background striking midnight, it is time for a new day—time to stop and then start over.

****

Go home and write the story
Go home and give the glory
To the brave men and women who are out there
Living in the dirt, feeling the hurt,
Dying for our freedom.

Breinigsville, PA USA
20 August 2009
222524BV00006B/1/P